678

6.50
4.00

A Critique of
Modern Textual Criticism

A Critique of
Modern Textual Criticism

Jerome J. McGann

The University of Chicago Press   Chicago & London

THE UNIVERSITY OF CHICAGO PRESS, CHICAGO 60637
THE UNIVERSITY OF CHICAGO PRESS, LTD., LONDON

©1983 by The University of Chicago
All rights reserved. Published 1983
Paperback edition 1985
Printed in the United States of America
94 93 92 91 90 89 88 87 86 85   2 3 4 5 6

LIBRARY OF CONGRESS CATALOGING IN PUBLICATION DATA

McGann, Jerome J.
  A critique of modern textual criticism.

  Includes bibliographical references and index.
    1. Criticism, Textual. I. Title.
  P47.M34   1983   801'.959   82-20151
  ISBN 0-226-55851-7 (cloth)
  ISBN 0-226-55852-5 (paper)

In short, let us provoke them—and our readers, and ourselves—to thought, which is the purest of scholarly pleasures; and I address this exhortation perhaps more to myself than to anyone else.

E. Talbot Donaldson

I began this discussion in the hope of clearing my own mind as well as others' on a rather obscure though not unimportant matter of editorial practice. I have done something to sort out my own ideas: others must judge for themselves. If they disagree, it is up to them to maintain some different point of view. My desire is rather to provoke discussion than to lay down the law.

W. W. Greg

Contents

Acknowledgments

Several of my friends and colleagues have helped and encouraged me in these studies, and have sometimes offered criticisms which forced me to think more carefully about some of the problems involved. I want particularly to thank, in this regard, Edward Brown, Cecil Lang, Michael Murrin, Lee Patterson, Mac Pigman, G. Thomas Tanselle, and Barry Weller. Finally, I am deeply grateful for the trenchant critique to which Peter Blayney subjected this work in one of its earlier incarnations. My debts to other critics and scholars, many of whom I have never met except through their published works, are scattered throughout these pages, sometimes invisibly, sometimes in ways that are only too apparent.

Introduction

This book is not a primer on textual criticism, nor even an introduction to a new model for textual criticism. Of the former we have a number which are perfectly adequate, and a few which are excellent. As for the latter, though I think such a work is necessary, I do not see that anyone is ready yet to produce it. Too much innovative and exploratory work is being done at the moment in all the relevant fields; attempting a synthesis at this time would be, therefore, premature. Happily, the best available guides to textual criticism, for example the books by Pasquali and West, already occupy positions which are sufficiently advanced that they can serve as reliable points of departure for the new work that is needed.[1] We do not rest content with these works now only because they approach the problems of textual criticism from a special and limited point of view.

These works, that is to say, deal with classical texts, where the methodological problems are usually very different from the ones which students of English vernacular scriptures have to face, most particularly in the modern periods; and my concern in this book is not with the works of antiquity. Good introductory guides to textual criticism in modern English language scriptures are not lacking, but none, in my view, takes account of certain fundamental critical problems of method and theory. In this respect they are all surpassed by

Pasquali and West, and even by Maas.[2] Of course, there are good reasons for this deficiency, and I shall be touching on these matters in the course of this work. But one in particular must be mentioned here: that the inadequacies in our basic views about the Textual Criticism of modern works have only recently become so apparent as to be unavoidable.

Introductions to a field of study are produced when scholars can command a generic treatment of the material. At certain times, however, the field will be seen to have eluded, in various ways (some will seem trivial, some important), the basic working premises of the discipline. At such times the traditional introductory guides will necessarily seem, in different respects, problematic, and the field will suddenly erupt with new vigor and activity. This is knowledge fighting for its life, as it were. At such periods scholars do not produce reliable guides because they are too busy exploring the fault lines of what they already know and experimenting with new models and ideas.

Textual criticism of the modern literatures is clearly living through such a time. This is partly why the field is so interesting at this moment, and why it is being worked by so many interesting minds, some of them textual specialists, some of them scholars who have been drawn into the discussions by the gravity (if the pun be permitted) of the situation. This book is, therefore, an introduction of sorts, but not an introduction to textual criticism. For the general scholarly reader it is (or means to be) an introduction to the issues and problems which textual critics are now struggling with. For the textual scholar it is (or means to be) a critical summary of the key areas of debate. Textual criticism is in the process of reconceiving its discipline, and this book's aim is to clarify those central issues which have emerged during the past ten years or so. For such is the period when the City came increasingly to discover that its normal services were subject to unusual disturbances and breakdown.

The problems first emerged in a general (and therefore an obviously serious) way as a debate over the aims and programs of the CEAA (the Center for Editions of American Authors, later called the Center for Scholarly Editions).[3] The programmatic statement of aims and purposes issued by the CEAA in 1977 provoked a series of hostile rejoinders, and these in turn served to catalyze a wide range of critical comment which has by no means come to an end (though it has grown less heated and polemical, and much more seriously critical).[4] Ultimately these discussions found a purchase in Shakespearean and Elizabethan studies, the area which has always been, for English scholars and for obvious reasons, the crucial one. The current swirl of interest around the text (or texts) of *King Lear* merely focuses the general debate now being engaged by Elizabethan and Shakespearean scholars.[5]

Let me briefly summarize the issues in their general historical frame of reference.[6] Samuel Johnson's remarks on the texts of Shakespeare, quoted below (pp.16-17), epitomize the initial stage of the discussion. Eighteenth-century critics of Shakespeare have not fared well for their efforts to "methodize" the bard's corpus, but those efforts were the fruit of a perception very like Johnson's: the state of the Shakespearean texts seemed so evil and corrupt that rational means had to be found which could deal with the problems. Eighteenth-century "reason" is, however, the most idiosyncratic of phenomena, so that although Shakespeare's works were laid under the authority of scholarly method, the methods were largely plural, personal, and (finally) unmethodical.

This situation prevailed until the emergence of the so-called New Bibliography, when the powerful and truly methodical approaches to textual criticism, developed in classical and biblical studies through the nineteenth-century, were finally adapted to Shakespearean and Elizabethan scholarship. This scholarly line reached its apogee in the work of Fredson Bowers and his followers, who carried to a finished form certain lines of thought developed by the New Bibliographers. Central to these views was the concept of the eclectic text. According to this line of argument, when scholars set about editing works of the past—and in particular when they are dealing with works for which we do not have an author's manuscript—they must develop methods for reconstituting the lost original document. Thus, from an examination of the two early and authoritative texts of *King Lear*, the 1608 Quarto and the 1623 Folio, the scholar will seek to educe an "eclectic" text of the play that will be, presumably, closer to "what Shakespeare originally wrote" than either of the early printed texts.[7]

The scholarly methods for producing eclectic texts quickly spread to all fields and areas, including those—for example, American literature—where original holograph manuscripts have survived. Many of the debates which take place around the programs of the CEAA/CSE involve the problems such a procedure necessarily creates. When the controversies began to break out in Shakespearean studies, however, the critical methods which looked to produce eclectic texts, and to search out the author's "lost original documents," were thrown into a state of general scholarly crisis. For if scholars were misguided in their assessments of the two original printed texts of *King Lear*—if, for example, these are not two *relatively corrupted* texts of a pure (but now lost) original, but two *relatively reliable* texts of two different versions of the play (as we now think)—then our general methods for dealing with such texts is called into serious question. Furthermore, since Shakespearean and Elizabethan studies constitute the central field in which our theories of textual criticism seek their ground, a crisis in that field involves a general crisis of the discipline.

This crisis is the subject I wish to explore here. Because Fredson Bowers is the scholar whose work brought the crisis to a head, his critical views will be a recurrent preoccupation of this study. He is the critic who brought to perfection, for editors of modern texts, the critical procedures we associate with the so-called Lachmann Method. How this came about, and what its results have been, are matters I shall want to take up in some detail. Almost equally important is the work of G. Thomas Tanselle, another imposing scholarly presence in the field. Tanselle's importance for these questions derives from the role he has consciously and resolutely assumed ever since the first signs of crisis began to appear in the discipline. That is to say, Tanselle's principal works have addressed themselves directly to the recent controversies and combatants. Tanselle has sought to moderate the conflicts and to salvage, by diplomatic accommodations, the basic methodologies handed down through the critical traditions. In the process he has played a number of useful roles, not the least of which—from my point of view—has been his ability to summarize and focus the central issues.

These conflicts and issues appear in their simplest and clearest forms when one encounters the following difference of opinion between leading textual authorities of our time.[8]

> When an author's manuscript is preserved, this has paramount authority, of course. Yet the fallacy is still maintained that since the first edition was proofread by the author, it must represent his final intentions and hence should be chosen as copy-text. Practical experience shows the contrary. . . . Thus the editor must choose the manuscript as his major authority, correcting

from the first edition only what are positive errors in the
accidentals of the manuscript. (Fredson Bowers)

Which brings us back to the first edition and to the
manuscript from which it was set. At first glance it
might seem that the manuscript will be the obvious
choice for copy-text. . . . But in most cases the editor
will choose as copy-text an early printed edition, not the
manuscript.
    This is a satisfactory conclusion, since for many
authors the actual writing of the manuscript. . .is a
means of composition, not an end. (Philip Gaskell)

What separates these views may seem small enough, and
perhaps it is true that only a pedant would or should be concerned about such matters. As so often happens, however, a
close study of the meaning of this difference of opinion
uncovers a series of fundamental questions which educators,
students of culture, and teachers of literature are always concerned with. Imbedded in that small difference are large
assumptions about the very nature of literary artifacts. In the
event, I found myself in closer agreement with Gaskell than
with Bowers; but what seemed to me more important, I
found myself understanding better the issues and problems
which were involved.
    Of course, the difference between Bowers and Gaskell
may be and often has been smoothed out when consensus
statements are sought after. For example, in April 1977 the
MLA's Center for Scholarly Editions (CSE) prepared an
"Introductory Statement" of editorial standards and guidelines
for workers in the field. This statement included the following
central paragraph.

    A primary requirement for any responsible edition is
    that it include a statement identifying the document

which supplies the copy-text—that is, the text which the editor is following as the basic text. When more than one text exists, a reasoned choice among them can be made only on the basis of a knowledge of their relationships with one another. The textual history of the material should therefore be presented in enough detail to allow the reader to follow the thinking that led the editor to a particular choice of copy-text and to particular evaluations of the relative authority of the other texts. It is frequently true that an author's completed manuscript, or—when the manuscript does not survive—the earliest printed edition based on it, reflects the author's intentions more fully than later editions or transcripts, in which printers' or copyists' corruptions are likely to have multiplied; in such cases, an editor producing a critical text would choose the early copy-text and would emend it to correct erroneous readings and to incorporate later variants that can be convincingly identified as genuine authorial revisions. But there are instances in which an author worked in such a way that a later text becomes a justifiable choice for copy-text; and there are situations in which an author can be said to have produced more than one "final" version of a work, any one or all of which an editor may decide to edit as separate entities. Each case must be examined independently in the light of all the available internal and external evidence; only then is an editor in a position to defend a specific choice of copy-text and to explain what categories of emendation (if any) are required. [9]

There was a time when I would have found this statement unexceptionable, but the things which I have seen I now can see no more. In one sense, of course, the statement is admirable, for it elucidates the fact that editorial problems vary from case to case, and that decisions can only be made when all relevant factors are taken into account. My own work editing Byron's poems proved the necessity of an ad hoc approach of this kind: the circumstances surrounding Byron's different works changed so often that the textual issues likewise showed wide variations. Not until very late in my own work, on Byron in particular, but in textual theory and method generally, was I able to see why this statement troubled my mind. Implicit in it are ideas about the nature of literary production and textual authority which so emphasize the autonomy of the isolated author as to distort our theoretical grasp of the "mode of existence of a literary work of art" (a mode of existence which is fundamentally social rather than personal). These ideas are grounded in a Romantic conception of literary production, and they have a number of practical consequences for the way scholars are urged to edit texts and critics are urged to interpret them. The ideas are also widespread in our literary culture, and since they continue to go largely unexamined in the fundamental ways that seem to me necessary, they continue to operate at the level of ideology. I have tried in this book to lift these issues out of that realm of ideology and into the realm of criticism, where knowledge can be advanced.

Readers familiar with the subject of this book will recognize many of the particular arguments I will be advancing. I have in fact borrowed shamelessly from the work of many scholars far more acute and learned than I, and I hope my appropriation of their studies has been adequately acknowledged. My own contributions to the advancement of this learning are limited to the following material and procedural matters. First, some of the examples and case studies offered here will not have been seen before. Second, the book tries to develop a fully elaborated argument for a socialized concept of authorship and textual authority. Third, and perhaps most significantly, the analysis is approached from a historical point of view, and with a firm sense that the issues raised here are intimately related to all aspects of scholarship and literary study. This approach, which used to be commonplace among philologians and textual critics, has lately fallen into some disuse, and the discipline has suffered as a consequence. My own view is that the explanation of textual criticism—hence, our understanding of how to do it, now or at any point—must not be sought after in the method per se, but in the history of the development of the method. Our critical knowledge of *texts* is advanced when we take such a historical approach; the situation is no different when our object is to understand better the disciplines we use.

Of course, the issues which this book deals with are not ordinarily thought to concern anyone but editors, bibliographers, and that small band of angels called textual critics. In writing it, however, I have deliberately tried to make its discussions accessible to critics and scholars generally. As a consequence, I may have sometimes brought topics forward which textual specialists may think tedious or unnecessary. Some elementary matters are taken up at a length which may not seem useful to the textualist, and on several occasions I have taken up the same or related subjects from several different angles, so that the knowledgeable textual scholar may find some of the discussions repetitive. I have tried to be severe with myself on these issues, and I must now say that what remains here seems to me essential, both for the textual specialist and the general critic. Textual critics remain relatively innocent of the large theoretical issues and problems which have recently come to light, principally, it seems to me, for two reasons. First, they do not normally see the problems except in terms of some local set of issues. The people who are most practically interested in these issues are ordinarily editors, and few editors are able to see their work and its attendant issues as part of a large and connected network of related issues and problems. Second, editors and even textual theorists of modern literatures have shown almost no interest in the general history of their discipline. As a result, the crisis facing the discipline is not normally seen within the context which would help to explain that crisis—or even make the crisis visible. I have therefore found it necessary to inquire after some familiar scholarly matters, but in contexts and relationships which even many textual specialists may not find so familiar.

Furthermore, the problems now facing editors and textual theorists of modern national scriptures expose a number of larger and more general problems, and these must concern all literary scholars and critics. This book is partly addressed to the general literary critic, as I have said, but that person equally lives and moves and has his being inside the most specialized editor or textual scholar. The issues raised in this book bear upon fundamental aspects of the theory of literature in general, including the theory of literary interpretation. Such matters form no part of these present discussions, however, nor should they do so. To take them up would only distract attention from my chief polemical conviction: that these issues in textual criticism and editorial theory are matters of general concern to the literary community.

Nevertheless, this book has been written with those larger issues very much in mind. We shall not begin to deal adequately with the problems currently facing editors and editorial theorists until we have reconceived the entire project of textual criticism for modern national scriptures. Certain shrewd literary critics have recently shown an interest in these larger matters—we hear much talk about "unstable texts," "unreliable texts," and *textualité*, and we often find interpretative essays playing ironically with those textual variants and textual versions which were normally of interest only to editors and textual critics (in the traditional sense).[10] This generalized interest observable in the larger field of literary studies can only be welcomed, since it promises the possibility that the schism between textual and interpretive studies, opened so long ago, may begin to be healed. The dawn is red with that promise.

First, however, we shall have to undertake a number of imperative scholarly tasks. Two of the foremost, in my view, are the following. We need to become fully conscious of the history of scholarship (not merely the history of criticism) from the late eighteenth century to the present, including the history of classical and biblical scholarship.[11] Second, we have to reimagine the central place which textual criticism occupies in literary studies. This book addresses itself to that second matter. The crisis in editorial theory, which is the particular focus of this work, must be explored first, since it is through that crisis that history has brought to our attention today the larger issues facing our discipline. This crisis finds its dialectical counterpart in certain areas of hermeneutics which currently preoccupy literary interpreters. But these latter subjects are already being explored by a variety of intelligent scholars, while the equally crucial, and deeply correspondent, crisis in editorial theory and practice has yet to receive a generic study. This book aims to open such a project. Its ultimate hope, and expectation, is that the crisis of two disciplines—in hermeneutics, on the one hand, and editorial method on the other—will not fail to bring about their destined appointment. When this happens, we may find that we have discovered again the ground of a comprehensive Textual Criticism — that *philologia perennis* known to certain great scholarly minds in the past, and that was renamed, not so very long ago, *Alterthumswissenschaft.*

Finally, although I am aware that this book takes up the most fugitive and cloistered of subjects, I have all along felt it to be an important topic as well, despite its specialized and perhaps even Lilliputian character. The subject and its demands have therefore chastened my mind considerably, and left me with fewer illusions about what we do when we study literary works. The book has its origins in the deepest sort of ignorance, when I hardly understood the true extent of my own ignorance. In the event, I read for the first time some of the works of Eichhorn, Herder, Humboldt, and Wolf, older scholars and critics who restored some perspective to my understanding of contemporary criticism, and whose astonishing grasp of textual studies has been continually before my eyes, not so much for what they knew as for their respect for knowledge itself, and for the humility which, as a consequence, marks all their work that I have read. In short, I have tried to write this little book in the spirit of a remark like the following by F. A. Wolf:

> I have truly done all that lay within my powers. . . . But this is a task worthy of many people's labors—of people who advance along different scholarly roads, and particularly of those who can measure the strength of human genius in poetry against the standard of their own genius, and who have an artistic judgment founded upon a knowledge of ancient literature: the Klopstocks, the Wielands, the Vosses.

> Feci quidem et ipse utrumque pro virili parte . . . ; sed haec complurium et diversa via ingredientium studiis digna cura est, in primis eorum, qui vim humani ingenii

in hoc genere metiri possunt ex suo ingenio, et iudicium
artis subactum habent antiquarum litterarum cogni-
tione, Klopstockiorum, Wielandorum, Vossiorum.[12]

1. Modern Textual Criticism:
A Schematic History

All current textual critics, whether they work on Homer, Langland, Shakespeare, or a Romantic poet like Byron, agree that to produce a critical edition entails an assessment of the history of the text's transmission with the purpose of exposing and eliminating errors. Ultimately, the object in view is the same in each case: to establish a text which, in the now universally accepted formulation, most nearly represents the author's original (or final) intentions.[13]

This critical commonplace has emerged gradually during the past two hundred years or so. It is a principle which assumes, quite correctly, that all acts of information transmission produce various sorts of corruption from the original material. Classical scholarship, which eventually produced the determinate breakthrough known as the Lachmann Method, established the basic rationale for the general procedures.[14] Lacking the author's original documents, possessing only a more or less extensive set of later manuscripts, the classical editor developed procedures for tracing the internal history of these late manuscripts. The aim was to work out textual errors by revealing the history of their emergence. Ultimately, the method sought to "clear the text" of its corruptions and, thereby, to produce (or approximate)—by subtraction, as it were—the lost original document, the "authoritative text."

These methods were soon applied to national scriptures of various kinds. In England, the New Bibliography centered

its work in Shakespeare, where the problems which the Lachmann Method was fashioned to deal with were in certain
important respects quite similar.[15] Samuel Johnson's famous
lament over the state of the Shakespearean texts contains a
neat formulation of the problem.

> The business of him that republished an ancient book is,
> to correct what is corrupt, and to explain what is
> obscure. To have a text corrupt in many places, and in
> many doubtful, is, among the authours that have writ-
> ten since the use of types, almost peculiar to Shak-
> espeare. Most writers, by publishing their own works,
> prevent all various readings, and preclude all conjectural
> criticism. Books indeed are sometimes published after
> the death of him who produced them, but they are
> better secured from corruptions than these unfortunate
> compositions. They subsist in a single copy, written or
> revised by the authour; and the faults of the printed
> volume can be only faults of one descent.
>
> But of the works of Shakespeare the condition has
> been far different: he sold them, not to be printed, but
> to be played. They were immediately copied for the
> actors, and multiplied by transcript after transcript,
> vitiated by the blunders of the penman, or changed by
> the affectation of the player; perhaps enlarged to intro-
> duce a jest, or mutilated to shorten the representation;
> and printed at last without the concurrence of the
> authour, without the consent of the proprietor, from
> compilations made by chance or by stealth out of the
> separate parts written for the theatre: and thus thrust
> into the world surreptitiously and hastily, they suffered
> another depravation from the ignorance and negligence
> of the printers, as every man who knows the state of the
> press in that age will readily conceive.

It is not easy for invention to bring together so many
causes concurring to vitiate a text. No other authour
ever gave up his works to fortune and time with so little
care: no books could be left in hands so likely to injure
them, as plays frequently acted, yet continued in
manuscript: no other transcribers were likely to be so little qualified for their task as those who copied for the
stage, at a time when the lower ranks of the people were
universally illiterate: no other editions were made from
fragments so minutely broken, and so fortuitously reun-
ited; and in no other age was the art of printing in such
unskilful hands.[16]

The state of the Shakespearean texts corresponded to the
state of the classical and biblical texts in this respect: in each
case the authorized documents were missing, so that critical
editors were faced with the problem of sorting through the
mediated texts which developed subsequently, in the scribal
process which preserved, disseminated, and reproduced the
lost original works. Of course, the Shakespearean problem
differed from the classical problem in two important ways.
First, the process of reproducing Shakespeare's lost original
documents was typographical rather than scribal. Second,
unlike the classical texts, the lost Shakespearean documents
were not radically separated in time from their subsequent
process of preservation and reproduction.[17] Stemmatics is a
complex problem in classical scholarship, whereas in Shakespearean studies it is normally a relatively straightforward
matter: the textual history in the latter case is, as we now say,
monogenous, whereas in the former it is polygenous.

These differentials necessitated some adjustments of the
Lachmann Method by Shakespearean scholars. Pollard,
McKerrow, and Greg were prominent initiators of these refor-
mulations, and their activities in the field established the

direction of the twentieth century's textual criticism of Shakespeare.[18] More than that, however, they exerted a powerful influence upon the textual criticism of all periods of our national scriptures. The influence has been most noticeable in the textual criticism of Restoration and eighteenth-century literature, and, more recently, of various nineteenth-century authors, both English and American. Indeed, these nineteenth-century instances have emerged as the focal point of most current problems with the theory of textual criticism.

In his celebrated essay "Some Principles for Scholarly Editions of Nineteenth-Century American Authors"[19] Fredson Bowers took the case of Hawthorne to lay down some rules for editing novels like *The Blithedale Romance*. This work is typical of the vast majority of works written and published in the modern periods: that is to say, it is a work for which we have the author's original manuscript. Thus, the classical problem which originally established the terms of modern textual criticism—the absence of the authoritative text—no longer pertains. Indeed, that fundamental and complex problem in classical studies—to find and remove textual contaminations—normally subsides in these cases to a secondary, if sometimes complex, operational task. Stemmatics and its related problems of emendation loom over the editors of classical as well as most medieval texts because the processes of textual transmission have been severely ruptured by time and circumstance.

Texts produced and reproduced in the earlier sixteenth and seventeenth centuries—pre-eminently Shakespeare's texts—raise special issues and problems, some of which I shall glance at in the following pages. My chief interest, however, lies with the texts produced and reproduced in the later modern (that is, the post-seventeenth-century) periods, for these texts have served to focus discussion of the theory of final intentions. Specifically, the theoretical interests of textual critics working largely in the modern periods have shifted from the field of stemmatics to the problems of copy-text.

This shift witnesses the profound influence which the earlier work of Fredson Bowers had upon the field of textual criticism. Bowers advanced a theory of final intentions in order to solve certain editorial problems which are typical of works typographically produced in the later modern periods. This theory was based upon a reading and interpretation of W. W. Greg's important essay "The Rationale of Copy-Text," where the main interest lies with Shakespeare and works produced in the early modern periods.

Bowers's altered focus upon the later modern periods, and particularly upon American books, has meant that he typically deals with works for which we have one or more of the author's pre-publication texts. These subjects lead him to the following argument, which I now quote in full.

> When an author's manuscript is preserved, this has paramount authority, of course. Yet the fallacy is still maintained that since the first edition was proofread by the author, it must represent his final intentions and hence should be chosen as copy-text. Practical experience shows the contrary. When one collates the manuscript of *The House of Seven Gables* against the first printed edition, one finds an average of ten to fifteen differences per page between the manuscript and the print, many of them consistent alterations from the manuscript system of punctuation, capitalization, spelling, and word-division. It would be ridiculous to argue that Hawthorne made approximately three to four thousand small changes in proof, and then wrote the manuscript of *The Blithedale Romance* according to the same system as the manuscript of the *Seven Gables*, a system that he had rejected in proof.

> A close study of the several thousand variants in
> *Seven Gables* demonstrates that almost every one can be
> attributed to the printer. That Hawthorne passed them
> in proof is indisputable, but that they differ from what
> he wrote in the manuscript and manifestly preferred is
> also indisputable. Thus the editor must choose the
> manuscript as his major authority, correcting from the
> first edition only what are positive errors in the acciden-
> tals of the manuscript.[20]

Here, though the textual problems are far removed from those faced by Lachmann, the influence of the classical approach is clear. Printing-house punctuation—the editorial intervention by a publisher or his agents between the author's manuscript and the published text—is regarded as a corruption of the authoritative text. It makes no difference, in Bowers's view, that the author oversaw and accepted this editorial intervention. As Bowers says a bit later in the essay,

> One is foolish to prefer a printing-house style. This dis-
> tinction is not theory, but fact. Hawthorne's punctua-
> tion, for example, is much more meaningful in respect
> to emphasis and to delicate matters of parenthesis and
> subordination than is the printing-house style in which
> *Seven Gables* and *The Blithedale Romance* appeared. In
> each book, the real flavor of Hawthorne, cumulatively
> developing in several thousand small distinctions, can be
> found only in the manuscript.[21]

This "theory of a critical edition"[22] is now widely accepted, and it indeed represents a reasonable approach to the choice of copy-text, especially when one reflects upon the historical development of the discipline. Bowers dismisses the chief alternative approach, "that since the first edition was proofread by the author, it must represent his final intentions and hence should be chosen as copy-text." This idea is a "fallacy . . . still maintained" in the teeth of what to Bowers seems manifest: that editorial intervention at the point of initial publication represents a process of deviation from the authoritative original, in fact, a process of corruption.

Bowers's views, then, continue to show the influence of the textual criticism developed in the field of classical studies. Hawthorne's early publisher, his editors, his printers are, for Bowers, entirely comparable to those older scribes who sought to preserve and transmit the classical texts, but who introduced, in the process, various contaminations. The business of the classical critic is to find and remove those corruptions, and the business of the critic of Hawthorne's texts is seen in the same way: to find and remove the corruptions and, by critical subtraction, to restore the sincerity of the authoritative text.[23]

This approach continues to dominate the current theory of textual criticism, though it has of course been challenged from various quarters, particularly by critics who work in the modern periods. The distinguished textual critic G. Thomas Tanselle recently surveyed, and rebutted, the chief lines of attack in an important essay. But the opposition has not been silenced, and Tanselle himself indicated certain key fault lines in the Bowers view.[24]

A vigorous line of dissent from Bowers has been carried by James Thorpe and Philip Gaskell, though Donald Pizer and others have raised some important objections of their own.[25] Tanselle's rebuttal of these dissenting lines is impressive partly because of Tanselle's personal tact, and partly because he is defending a position whose strength lies in its logical coherence and self-consistency. Again and again Tanselle parries the opponents of Bowers by pointing to the irrelevance of the objections for the dominant theory, or to the theoretical and methodological contradictions which appear in the arguments and positions of the dissenting critics. Such contradictions proliferate, it is clear, at least partly because the dissenting positions are not founded upon a carefully articulated theoretical structure. As we shall see later, the contradictions are also the result of the compromised nature of the dissenting views, which have not been able to divorce themselves from certain key aspects of the views they are attacking. This, too, as we shall also see, represents failure of theory.[26]

Up to now I have been discussing this critical dialogue at a rather high level of abstraction, principally in order to expose the general shape of the critical debate, rather than the precise areas of conflict. We will need to keep the larger view in mind, since it is my contention that the dissenting line, though lacking the theoretical rigor of the Bowers position, preserves the latter in a state of crisis by raising over and over again vexing practical problems which the Bowers line cannot easily deal with. In other words, the dissenting line involves alternative theoretical grounds which it has not yet articulated self-consciously in the way that Bowers has done.

2. Modern Textual Criticism: The Central Problems

Let us begin the discussion again, this time at a more analytic level. Present-day textual criticism, as we have seen, is the descendant of the earlier historical critics of biblical and classical texts, among whom Lachmann is by common consent the most notable. Out of this early work in classical philology emerged two of the three principal areas of current interest: the theory of the critical edition, and the theory of the copy-text. The second of these has been a special preoccupation of those inheritors of the Lachmann Method, the New Bibliographers. When the latter began to concern themselves with textual problems of the more modern periods, they opened up the third area in which debate is now frequently joined: the problem (or the theory) of final authorial intentions. We will consider each of these matters in turn. These discussions will eventually force us to consider a fourth subject, the theory of the nonspecialist or modernized edition. Largely a neglected concern of modern textual criticism, the topic will prove a crucial one for sorting out the problems which current textual theory has discovered for itself.

THE THEORY OF THE CRITICAL EDITION

The attempt by classical philologists to recover, or approximate by historical reconstruction, the lost original works of ancient authors produced a "theory of the critical edition." The chief device for constructing such an edition was then, and still is, the systematic collation of all the relevant texts of the work in question. Out of the collation emerges an analytic picture of the work's historical passage, and, as a natural consequence, the critical opportunity of removing the errors consequent upon such a passage.

The production of this collation entails as well the development of a textual stemma, that is, a summary analysis of the historical relations of the various specific texts of the work in question. The stemma is an especially important tool for an editor when he is choosing his copy-text, which is in a "general sense" an "early text of a work which an editor [selects] as the basis of his own."[27] The copy-text, in fact, permits the critic to sort out and arrange the collations. In a properly critical edition, the editor will produce a critical text which is based upon the copy-text but into which has been introduced a series of emendations and corrections. These changes are designed to bring the critical text into as close an approximation as possible with the author's no longer extant work. A textual apparatus accompanies the critical text, and this contains as complete a record as is possible of the textual variants which have emerged from the collation of the documents. It is this apparatus which displays the "history" of the text.

The Theory of Copy-text

The above general theory of the critical edition is now accepted, with minor variations and modifications, by all textual critics and critical editors. But the special problems of editing Shakespeare and other English authors of the early-modern periods led Greg to develop a "rationale of copy-text," which is explicitly designed to deal mainly with problems raised by certain national scriptures produced in the early modern typographical periods. As Greg put the matter:

> If I am right in the view that I am about to put forward, the classical theory of the "best" or "most authoritative" manuscript, whether it be held in a reasonable or in an obviously fallacious form, has really nothing to do with the English theory of "copy-text" at all.[28]

The New Bibliography was interested in considering more closely how a critic was to choose, among the possible options, one specific text which would serve him as his base text or copy-text. On what grounds should one make such a choice, what was a coherent theory of copy-text? Greg's interest in this question led him to produce his famous essay.

According to Greg, in the context of a monogenous textual stemma—that is, in the situation which one frequently encounters in a bibliographical context, but only rarely in a scribal one—textual critics can and should approach the problem of copy-text in a systematic way. Greg followed "the modern editorial practice [of choosing] whatever extant text may be supposed to represent most nearly what the author wrote and to follow it with the least possible alteration."[29] But Greg went on to make his famous distinction between accidentals and substantives in order to set up a rationale for the use of the copy-text:

> Since, then, it is only on grounds of expediency, and in consequence either of philological ignorance or of linguistic circumstances, that we select a particular original as our copy-text, I suggest that it is only in the matter of accidentals that we are bound (within reason) to follow it, and that in respect of substantive readings we have exactly the same liberty (and obligation) of choice as has a classical editor, or as we should have were it a modernized text that we were preparing.[30]

Greg arrives at this formulation because he wants to define a standard of authority between early texts and later revised texts (including those which carry genuine authorial revisions). That standard lies in the so-called accidentals, which will be, in the earliest monogenous textual forms, necessarily closest to "the author's original in so far as the general form of the text is concerned." Because this is the case, the critic's copy-text must be that text in the monogenous series which is historically closest to the author's lost original, for to displace it in favor of a reprint, whether authoritatively revised or not, means receding at least one step further from the general form of the author's original.

> The true theory is, I contend, that the copy-text should govern (generally) in the matter of accidentals, but that the choice between substantive readings belongs to the general theory of textual criticism and lies altogether beyond the narrow principle of the copy-text. Thus it may happen that in a critical edition the text rightly chosen as copy may not by any means be the one that supplies most substantive readings in cases of variation. The failure to make this distinction and to apply this principle has naturally led to too close and too general a reliance upon the text chosen as basis for an edition, and there has arisen what may be called the tyranny of the copy-text, a tyranny that has, in my opinion, vitiated much of the best editorial work of the past generation.[31]

This famous passage represents what Greg earlier called "the English theory of copy-text," which Greg correctly recognized as the consequence of the developing work of the New Bibliographers. McKerrow supplied Greg with his initial formulation of the theory, but Greg's view was that McKerrow "relapsed into heresy" out of a fear of "conceding too much to eclecticism." The true "English theory" of copy-text means to draw a distinction between a text's substantives and its accidentals, and to argue that whereas the critic should choose "the earliest 'good' print as copy-text" and should follow that in its accidentals, he should be prepared to deviate from the copy-text in the matter of substantive readings.[32]

Greg's argument, we must observe, leaves aside altogether the question of "the choice between substantive readings," nor does it address directly the question of textual "versions," as they are now called. When "there is more than one substantive text of comparable authority," or as we should say when there is more than one version, Greg owns that the choice between them will be an arbitrary and expedient matter. Greg's purpose here is to free the editor from the tyranny of a copy-text, "to uphold his liberty of judgement" and discretion when decisions have to be made: "In the case of rival substantive editions the choice between substantive variants is...generally independent of copy-text."[33]

At this point we should recall that Greg's rationale makes no appeal to any concept of author's intentions (whether original or final). When editing a work, as Tanselle has observed, "It is not necessary to have a copy-text at all in the strict sense of the term which Greg develops."[34] The term can be used in a general sense to refer to the editor's chosen base text or version, of course, but in Greg's determination copy-text is a device for helping an editor choose between "indifferent readings." Tanselle elucidates the theory of copy-text economically.

> Generally speaking, an editor has less to go on when judging variants in punctuation and spelling than when judging variants in wording, and for that reason the text chosen as copy-text often supplies most of the punctuation and spelling for the critical text. But the editor is

free, of course, to make rational decisions regarding
spelling and punctuation when the evidence permits;
conversely, variants in wording can sometimes seem
indifferent, and the impasse is resolved by adopting the
copy-text reading. . . . [A] copy-text is simply the text
most likely to provide an authorial reading . . . at points
of variation where one cannot otherwise reach a
decision.[35]

This seems to me an accurate translation of Greg's position.
As we shall see, however—and as the passages I quoted from
Bowers show—whereas Greg never sought to interpret his
rationale in terms of authorial intentions, this is precisely
what Bowers would later propose. As a consequence, the
theory of authorial intentions was formulated not merely as
an explanation of the rationale of copy-text, but as a rule
which would be asked to govern both the choice of the copy-
text and the choice of the textual version as well.

The Problem (and Theory) of Final Intentions

Greg's theory of copy-text was developed to deal primarily
with certain problems in Elizabethan bibliography, though it
obviously has a general bearing on scribal texts as well. The
theory grew from Greg's awareness that when texts were produced in typographical forms in the early modern periods,
their orthography—what Greg called "the general form of the
text"—was subject to frequent and odd changes (so-called
modernizations) as the work passed through the hands of the
printers and publishers. In an unpublished essay which takes
up this matter, Peter Blayney explains the situation lucidly:

If the fourth paragraph of "The Rationale" is read with
uniform attention it becomes quite clear that there is
one overriding reason why the author's (usually lost)

manuscript is held up as the final authority for accidentals. Quite simply, before the eighteenth century no other possible "standard" for accidentals exists.

Before 1650, while "house style" varied from printing house to printing house and from compositor to compositor, rapidly changing "fashions" in orthography can be seen affecting the whole of the London printing trade. . . . Greg never put it in so many words, but was well aware that *all* the compositors of the First Folio (and their contemporaries) scattered punctuation and capitals around in a profusion seldom matched even in the 18th century. In this respect they all differed from *all* the compositors who set Shakespeare's Quartos. . . . The point is that one can legitimately define a hefty percentage of the seemingly arbitrary changes that distinguish (say) a 1605 reprint from its 1595 copy as *modernizations*. And it was modernization that Greg was trying to minimize.[36]

Greg himself refers to these matters only by implication, or obliquely—as in the following passage: "The thesis I am arguing is that the historical circumstances of the English language make it necessary to adopt in formal matters the guidance of some particular early text."[37] The "historical circumstances of the English language" and its processes of transmission led Greg to formulate his rationale for the editing of early modern texts. Subsequent editors and theorists have gone on to apply Greg's rationale to works of later periods when, in Blayney's words, "there *was* such a thing as 'standard' orthography."

Under these new textual circumstances, new problems have emerged, the most pressing of which has come to seem the problem of the author's final intentions. Greg's theory can be made to deal reasonably well with such problems in circumstances where the author's original text is not preserved.

But in more recent periods, and especially in those which saw the emergence of modern textual criticism itself, authorial texts abound: draft copies, corrected drafts, fair copies (holograph, or amanuensis copies with or without autograph corrections for the press), proofs (uncorrected or corrected, sometimes by the author, sometimes by his editors). In these circumstances, a theory of final intentions has emerged out of the Lachmann-Greg tradition which has received its most eloquent formulation in the work of Fredson Bowers, whose normative statements on the matter I have already quoted.

I must point out, in passing, that in so far as Greg concerned himself with the problem of author's intentions at all, his position was typically discretionary: "authority is never absolute, but only relative," he observed when he was beginning to attack "the tyranny of the copy-text."[38] Of course, Greg can speak of "the author's original text," and he has in fact endorsed the following editorial principle: "It is . . . the modern editorial practise to choose whatever extant text may be supposed to represent most nearly what the author wrote and to follow it with the least possible alteration.[39] Nevertheless, when he laid aside the problem of textual versions in his theory of copy-text, he was implicitly laying aside the problem of authorial intentions as well. The locus of his special concern was a period when such problems did not rise up with the urgency or in the forms which Bowers and others have encountered.

Bowers's appeals to Greg and the previous traditions of textual criticism represent an effort to support Bowers's theory of authorial intentions by an appeal to Greg's rationale for editing early modern texts. But special problems appear when textual critics seek to apply Greg's rationale to texts, especially modern ones, which come down to us in forms that trace back to preserved original manuscripts and other pre-publication documents.[40] Bowers's position—that an editor must choose, other things being equal, the earliest in the surviving series of completed texts—is based upon the idea that the original in such a series will be closest to the author's final intentions, will be least contaminated by nonauthorial interventions—in particular, by nonauthoritative forms in the so-called accidentals.

Critics have repeatedly attacked this position on the matter of the accidentals, and have argued, in various ways, that the formal features of the authorial manuscripts—even printer's copy manuscripts—do not necessarily lie closest to the author's final intentions. In many cases—Gaskell and Thorpe give a number of typical ones—the first printed edition seems to exert at least as strong a claim to author's final intentions as the author's manuscript; and various particular cases have been raised to show that other textual constitutions—corrected proofs, later revised editions, and so forth—might reasonably claim to represent, in formal as well as in substantive matters, the author's final intentions.

Tanselle has vigorously rebutted these positions—more on that matter in a moment—but what he and most of the parties to the debate have thus far failed to emphasize is that the problems being raised are historically peculiar to circumstances where critics and editors have inherited an unprecedented amount of early textual material and related documentation. Under such conditions the critic is often able to follow the process of literary production through all its principal stages, and from the vantage of all the principal persons engaged in the process. Byron's poetry abounds in illustrative examples, but his case is merely prototypical. Nevertheless, a critic facing the massive textual documentation for a work like *The Giaour*—multiple manuscripts, multiple corrected and uncorrected proofs, a trial edition, a whole series of early editions at least three of which are known to have been proofed and revised by Byron—finds it difficult to accept the idea that one of these texts, and presumably an early manuscript, represents the author's final intentions. The case typifies what Hans Zeller has recently suggested: that texts frequently exist in several versions no one of which can be said to constitute itself the "final" one.[41]

Zeller has in mind famous cases like *The Prelude*, the special problems of which are sometimes handled in special critical formats, such as the facing-page edition. But the example of *The Giaour*—or *Childe Harold*, or *Don Juan*, or any number of Byron's other works—raises the problem of multiple versions beyond the capacity of a facing-page compromise. If, as Tanselle says, "the aim of the editor is to establish the text as the author wished to have it presented to the public,"[42] the case of Byron's works can stand as an exemplary one for a host of others: that is, many works exist of which it can be said that their authors demonstrated a number of different wishes and intentions about what text they wanted to be presented to the public, and that these differences reflect accommodations to changed circumstances, and sometimes to changed publics.[43]

Donald Pizer recently brought a similar objection to the Bowers theory of final intentions. Tanselle's answer to Pizer needs to be quoted here because it helps to illuminate the special character of the crisis facing the current theory of final intentions. Pizer argues that a modern critical editor may want to choose as copy-text a first edition rather than some prepublication text in those cases where author, publisher, and house editor worked closely in the production of the work. Tanselle counters Pizer in this way.

What appears in a prepublication form of a text is

normally a better representation of the author's habits than what appears in a first printing, and the text of a fair-copy manuscript or typescript reflects the author's intention, whether or not it turns out to be his final intention in every respect. It is true, as Pizer says, that choosing "an early copy-text encourages a frame of mind which requires later variants to 'prove themselves' as authorial rather than as editorial or printer's variants"; but such would seem to be the safest course in most instances, since the author's responsibility for a later reading—especially in accidentals—is normally less certain than his responsibility for an early one. Of course, such editorial caution may occasionally produce a text reflecting "an author's discarded rather than final intentions," but at least it reflects his, rather than someone else's, intentions. The editor's critical judgment—his literary taste exercised in the light of his intimate knowledge of the author and all known relevant external evidence—must finally determine the case; and there is nothing in Greg's theory to prevent him, on this basis, from deciding that the later variants have indeed "proved themselves." If, however, he starts from the assumption that the author and the publisher's editor are creative collaborators, he will, to be sure, produce an unmodernized text—in the sense that it reflects the author's period—but it may be far from the text which the author wished (finally, or at any other time).[44]

First, a practical point. It is true that an editor making Pizer's choice may produce a text which is "far from the text which the author wished" to have presented to the public. True—but, by the same token, an editor making Tanselle's or Bowers's choice is equally liable to the danger of producing a text which the author would never have wanted the public to see. The latter is an especially clear and present danger when one chooses to edit some prepublication version of a work, for obvious reasons. In each case a danger exists which must be met by the acuteness and skill of the individual editor, for—in *any* case—the best of imaginable strategies will collapse if the tactics are blundered. Certainly the Bowers *theory* of final intentions will be no protection under the circumstances detailed by Pizer. Such circumstances, needless to say, are common in the more modern periods—indeed, they are the rule.

The second point to be made goes to the issue of "intentions" generally. Following Bowers, Tanselle argues that if their "editorial caution" is open to the danger of choosing less-than-final intentions, "at least" it will capture the author's rather than someone else's intentions. One must note, simply in passing, that the authorial intentions marked in prepublication manuscripts will often represent in only the most tentative way what an author wished to have presented to the public, certainly in the matter of accidentals, and often of substantives as well. But this ambiguity in the concept of author's intention conceals an even more crucial problem in the Bowers's theory of final intentions. Once again it is a historically specific problem and appears in circumstances where the textual critic has in his possession, at the outset of his work, the early authoritative (prepublication) documents.

Tanselle's belief that the theory of copy-text will ensure an edition that "reflects [the author's], rather than someone else's, intentions" assumes that any editorial intervention at the work's point of origin constitutes a contamination of the authoritative text. But Pizer, like Thorpe, Gaskell, and others, has shown what everyone recognizes to be the historical facts: the production of books, in the later modern periods especially, sometimes involves a close working relationship between the author and various editorial and publishing professionals associated with the institutions which serve to transmit literary works to the public. To regard the work done by such institutions as a contamination of authorized material is to equate the editorial work done by an author's original publishing institutions and the (historically belated) editorial work done by the scribes of ancient texts. The original theory of the critical edition was developed to find and remove the contaminations inadvertently produced by those textual transmitters, and Greg's rationale represented a special variation on that theory, one designed to take account of the peculiar typographical conditions which prevailed before the eighteenth century. But the theory of final intentions, though a corollary derivative from the initial theory of the critical text and its special variant, has been asked to perform the same function under conditions which are structurally far different.

The scholarly consequences of this hegemonic use of the theory of final intentions are far reaching, and they extend ultimately to the way we read and comprehend literary works, and not merely to how we edit their texts. More immediately, the consequence has been to retard the development of the theory of textual criticism. Important critics and theorists continue to maintain the dominance of Bowers's theories even when the empirical evidence demonstrates, from many different quarters, that those theories are not adequate under certain circumstances. It is certainly true, as Tanselle has argued, that these theories are the most powerful and coherent that we currently possess; indeed, their continuing power resides in their coherence and methodological consistency, as Tanselle has also argued. Still, the empirical challenges to the theory raised by various learned voices argue that serious problems underlie the theory of final intentions when it is applied to a certain large class of (typically) modern works. But the fact that these challenges have remained largely empirical in character testifies as well to the absence of any substantial theoretic critique.

3. The Ideology of Final Intentions

Such a critique will only become possible when we are able to see more clearly the ideology which supports the concept of final intentions. We begin by returning briefly to a passage in Greg's famous essay where he summarizes his position.

> The thesis I am arguing is that the historical circumstances of the English language make it necessary to adopt in formal matters the guidance of some particular early text. If the several extant texts of a work form an ancestral series, the earliest will naturally be selected since this will not only come nearest to the author's original in accidentals, but also (revision apart) most faithfully preserve the correct readings where substantive variants are in question.[45]

This statement shows the special circumstances which Greg's theory was constructed to meet. When he speaks of several texts that "form an ancestral series," the monogenous pattern of Shakespearean texts—as opposed to the problems facing the editors of polygenous texts, such as Chaucer's—shows through very clearly. Furthermore, when Greg speaks of "author's original" we encounter a formulation which his inheritors—for present purposes, we will instance Bowers—will consistently revise and depart from. Bowers's summary of Greg's position is interesting in this context.

> Greg distinguished between the authority of the substan-
> tives and of the forms, or accidentals, assumed by these
> substantives. If only the first edition, set from
> manuscript, has authority, as being the closest in each of
> these two respects to the author's lost manuscript, then
> both authorities are combined in one edition. On the
> other hand, a revised edition may alter the authority of
> some of the substantives; but the transmission of the
> author's accidentals through the hands, and mind, of
> still another compositor destroys the authority of these
> features of the first edition, set from manuscript.[46]

This passage comes near the beginning of Bowers's famous
essay which we quoted from earlier. One notices here that he
does not speak of either "original" or "final" intentions. He
does not choose either term, in this place, because he is in the
midst of a demonstration which will lead him beyond Greg's
formulation ("author's original") to his own special variation
upon it. Thus, when Bowers does finally come to apply
Greg's theory to the editing of modern American authors,
where prepublication textual states are commonly extant, he
argues the theory of final intentions, as we have seen. In fact,
he and others are brought to use this term "final intentions"
precisely when the editorial problem shifts from the seventeenth to the nineteenth century. In Bowers's essays on
seventeenth-century editing problems—for example, in his
"Current Theories of Copy-Text, With an illustration from
Dryden,"—the concept of final intentions never appears.[47] It
manifestly has no relevance.

The theory of final intentions is an effort to deal systematically with a recurrent problem faced by the editors of
certain sorts of text. However, because the theory emerged
through the Lachmann-Greg tradition of critical editing, it

preserved certain features of earlier textual theories which were irrelevant to the new sets of problems. The theory of final intentions aims to provide a rule for the choice of a text under circumstances where several apparently fully authoritative texts exist. In Greg's terms, the theory attempts to provide a rationale not merely for emendation and correction procedures, but for choosing between "particular substantive editions" as well.[48] The theory develops because Greg's copy-text of rule—"the earliest" or first edition—becomes a "later" text when the ancestral series is invaded by still earlier, prepublication forms. In such a situation Bowers, Tanselle, and the many inheritors of Greg continue to follow his line of reasoning, and argue that the author's manuscript—because it is earliest in the ancestral series of monogenous texts—assumes the highest authority when the issue of copy-text is being met. We have already heard Bowers speak to this point. Tanselle's statement on the matter is interesting not because he follows Bowers, but because his argument takes the same form of thought, and clearly shows the continuing influence of Greg.

> Greg's rationale, pointing out the usual deterioration of a text (particularly its accidentals) from one manuscript or edition to another, leads the editor back to the fair-copy manuscript or the earliest extant text which follows it.[49]

Tanselle concludes in a way that is typical of his critical style, which is generally more cautious and less dismissive than Bowers's: "in the absence of additional evidence, the author's manuscript should be taken as a safer guide than the printed text to his intentions regarding accidentals."[50] But Tanselle's formulation, like Bowers's, betrays an innovative reading of Greg's famous essay. Tanselle and Bowers both speak of author's intentions when they discuss the rationale of copy-text, whereas Greg's essay never dealt with the problem of authorial intentions at all.

The rationale behind this extension of Greg's theory is not difficult to see. Faced with situations where an editor has to decide between numerous authoritative documents, between numerous textual versions whether in monogenous or polygenous forms, the editor cannot lay aside, as Greg had laid aside, the problem of the choice of a text at every level. Bowers faced this issue squarely, and he appropriated Greg's analysis of early modern typographical problems in order to formulate and argue for a theory of authorial intentions.

Now underlying all such formulations, but particularly those which erect a theory of final intentions out of the theory of copy-text, the concept of the autonomy of the creative artist can be seen to be assumed. Textual critics who had to deal with ancient writings, and especially with classical and biblical authors, came to see through their philological studies how these authors and their works had been isolated from the present by the very process—textual transmission—which delivered them over to the present. The ancient works were alienated from the present not so much in their distance from us as in the interruption of our view caused by the corrupting process of transmission. To be put in touch with these authors and their works, the historical method proposed not an elimination of the distance but a clearing of the view: take away the textual contaminants, remove the interfering scribal and typographical presence, and the autonomous original will appear before us.

This desire to bring into view what has been obscured by historical processes—to repair the wrecks of history by using a historical method—moved into a new and very different phase with the intentionalist interpreters of Greg's rationale

Having learned the lesson that authors who wish to make contact with an audience are fated, by laws of information theory, to have their messages more or less seriously garbled in the process, textual critics proposed to place the reader in an unmediated contact with the author. This project is of course manifestly impossible, a Heisenbergian dilemma, since some form of mediation is always occurring, not least in the editions produced by critical editors of various persuasions. Nevertheless, though everyone today recognizes this inherent limitation on all acts of communication, the idea persists in textual studies that a regression to authorial manuscripts will by itself serve to reduce textual contamination.

Two points must be made. In the first place, such a regression will not necessarily reduce contamination, but it will necessarily situate it differently. Furthermore, if printed forms follow manuscripts in the ancestral series, and if they are thereby fated to introduce fresh contamination in the process of transmission, they equally acquire the potential for decontamination, as the very project of textual criticism demonstrates. Author's works are typically clearer and more accessible when they appear in print. Besides, when an author is himself involved in the printing of his manuscript—when he proofs and edits—then the printed form will necessarily represent what might be called his final intentions, or "the text as the author wished to have it presented to the public." This position has been frequently maintained in actual practice, though Bowers heaps contempt upon it. It underlies Gaskell's untheorized rule that "in most cases the editor will choose as copy-text an early printed edition, not the manuscript."[51]

But a second point must be made that is even more fundamental, for it approaches the theory of final intentions via an exposure of its ideological assumptions. Gaskell and

Thorpe are prominent among those who argue, as Tanselle puts it, "that the author's intention encompasses the activities which take place in the step from manuscript (or typescript) to print and that the intention is not 'final' until the text conforms to the standards which will make it publishable."[52] Unlike Bowers, Tanselle feels the force of this argument, but he rejects it in the end because—as he argues elsewhere—"an author's manuscript stands a better chance of reflecting his wishes in accidentals than does a printed text."[53]

One may note in passing that an author's intentions toward his manuscript may be quite different—have special aims and reflect special circumstances—from his intentions toward his published text. Each may represent what Zeller has called a "different version." But this is by the way. What needs to be emphasized is Tanselle's idea that in matters of textual publication the author must be considered an autonomous authority. In this view, the textual critic is urged to produce an edition which most nearly reflects the author's autonomously generated text, and the critical editor will seek this goal even if that text is not one which the author published or could have had published.

This is a theory of textual criticism founded in a Romantic ideology of the relations between an author, his works, his institutional affiliations, and his audience. It stands in the sharpest contrast with the theory implicit in the following statement by James Thorpe.

> Various forces are always at work thwarting or modifying the author's intentions. The process of preparing the work for dissemination to a public (whether that process leads to publication in printed form or production in the theatre or preparation of scribal copies) puts the work in the hands of persons who are professionals in the execution of the process. Similarly, the effort to

recover a work of the past puts it in the hands of professionals known as textual critics, or editors. In all of these cases, the process must be adapted to the work at hand, and the work to the process. Sometimes through misunderstanding and sometimes through an effort to improve the work, these professionals substitute their own intentions for those of the author, who is frequently ignorant of their craft. Sometimes the author objects and sometimes not, sometimes he is pleased, sometimes he acquiesces, and sometimes he does not notice what has happened. The work of art is thus always tending toward a collaborative status, and the task of the textual critic is always to recover and preserve its integrity at that point where the authorial intentions seem to have been fulfilled.[54]

One must add to this—to keep the factual record clear—that authors sometimes positively seek the collaboration of publishers and their house editors in establishing the verbal format of their works. Byron is an exemplary instance of this case. Indeed, not only did Byron ask his press editor—chiefly William Gifford—for help in the final stages of revision, he even accepted the textual interventions of his chief amanuensis, Mary Shelley. When she copied works like Canto 3 of *Childe Harold* and the various cantos of *Don Juan*, she would regularly introduce alterations—mostly minor—into her copy. When Byron corrected this copy he would sometimes accept her changes and sometimes return to the original reading. Such instances of "collaboration" abound in all periods of literary production, as everyone recognizes, and I shall return to the Mary Shelley-Byron case a bit later.

But the collaboration of the author with the institutions of publishing is an activity which cannot be adequately understood if we focus merely on the textual evidence of such cooperative processes. Because literary works are

fundamentally social rather than personal or psychological
products, they do not even acquire an artistic form of being
until their engagement with an audience has been determined. In order to secure such an engagement, literary works
must be produced within some appropriate set of social institutions, even if it should involve but a small coterie of ama-
teurs. Blake perfectly exemplifies this fact about the nature of
literary work precisely because he tried to produce his own
work in deliberate defiance of his period's normal avenues of
publication. Blake retreated to a method of literary production which antedated even the patronage system of the
eighteenth century. And as for the commercial system of his
own day, this was an institution from which Blake early
sought to gain his independence. His project is implicit in
The Marriage of Heaven and Hell, and explicit in his 1793
"Prospectus."[55]

TO THE PUBLIC October 10, 1793
The Labours of the Artist, the Poet, the Musician, have
been proverbially attended by poverty and obscurity;
this was never the fault of the Public, but was owing to
a neglect of means to propagate such works as have
wholly absorbed the Man of Genius. Even Milton and
Shakespeare could not publish their own works.

    This difficulty has been obviated by the Author of
the following productions now presented to the Public;
who has invented a method of Printing both Letter-press
and Engraving in a style more ornamental, uniform,
and grand, than any before discovered, while it produces
works at less than one fourth of the expense.

    If a method of Printing which combines the Painter
and the Poet is a phenomenon worthy of public attention, provided that it exceeds in elegance all former
methods, the Author is sure of his reward.

* * *

The following are the Subjects of the several Works now published and on Sale at Mr. Blake's, No. 13, Hercules Buildings, Lambeth.

* * *

No Subscriptions for the numerous great works now in hand are asked, for none are wanted; but the Author will produce his works, and offer them to sale at a fair price.

Later—and specifically when he came under the influence of William Hayley—Blake swerved from his early radical project and sought to have his works published and distributed in the normal fashion.

The Profits arising from Publications are immense & I now have it in my power to commence publication with many very formidable works, which I have finish'd & ready. A Book price half a guinea may be got out at the Expense of Ten pounds & its almost certain profits are 500 G. I am only sorry that I did not know the methods of publishing years ago, & this is one of the numerous benefits I have obtain'd by coming here, for I should never have known the nature of Publication unless I had known H. & his connexions & his method of managing. It now would be folly to venture publishing.

New Vanities, or rather new pleasures, occupy my thoughts. New profits seem to arise before me so tempting that I have already involved myself in engagements that preclude all possibility of promising any thing. I have, however, the satisfaction to inform you that I have Myself begun to print an account of my various Inventions in Art, for which I have procured a Publisher.[56]

Blake's interest in working with, rather than apart from, the
publishing institution of his period was actively pursued
between 1803-8, but in the end withered because of the special character of his works. His letter to Dawson Turner of 9
June 1818 reflects his decision, in the final period of his life,
to accept what was a fatality imposed upon him from the
start, and by the very nature of his artistic productions.

> Sir,
> I send you a List of the different Works you have done
> me the honour to enquire after—unprofitable enough to
> me, tho' Expensive to the Buyer. Those I Printed for Mr
> Humphry are a selection from the different Books of
> such as could be Printed without the Writing, tho' to
> the Loss of some of the things. For they when Printed
> perfect accompany Poetical Personifications & Acts,
> without which Poems they never could have been Exe-
> cuted.

	s.	d.	
America. . . . 18 Prints folio	5	5	0
Europe . . . . 17 do. folio	5	5	0
Visions & . . . 8 do. folio	3	3	0
Thel. . . . . . 6 do. Quarto	2	2	0
Songs of Innocence 28 do. Octavo	3	3	0
Songs of Experience 26 do. Octavo	3	3	0
Urizen . . . . 28 Prints Quarto	5	5	0
Milton . . . . 50 do. Quarto	10	10	0
12 Large Prints, Size of Each about 2 feet by 1 & 1/2			
Historical & Poetical			
Printed in Colours . . Each	5	5	0

These last 12 prints are unaccompanied by any writing.
The few I have Printed & Sold are sufficient to have

gained me great reputation as an Artist, which was the
chief thing Intended. But I have never been able to produce a Sufficient number for a general Sale by means of
a regular Publisher. It is therefore necessary to me that
any Person wishing to have any or all of them should
send me their Order to Print them on the above terms,
& I will take care that they shall be done at least as well
as any I have yet Produced.[57]

When Blake assumed the roles of author, editor, illustra-
tor, publisher, printer, and distributor, he was plainly aspiring
to become a literary institution unto himself. Unfortunately,
he could not also assume the role of one crucial component
of that institution as it existed in his period: the reviewer. As
a consequence, his work reached only a small circle of his
contemporaries. Also, his productive processes were such that
he could not mass produce his works, so that his fame, his
full appreciation and influence, had to wait upon his death,
and the intervention of a number of important persons who
never even knew him. The mechanical reproduction of his
rare original works was a final, splendid insult to the equally
splendid principles of a genius. Had that insult never been
delivered, Blake would have been no more than one of those
who "bare of laurel . . . live, dream, and die."

When Keats wrote those words in order to distinguish
between the poet and the inarticulate visionary (see "The Fall
of Hyperion," lines 1-18), he meant to show that imaginative
power needs a medium of communication. In social circumstances, and especially in the modern periods of mechanical reproduction, Keats's "fine spell of words" is a metaphor
only, for words do not by themselves constitute a system of
communication. Keats's "warm scribe my hand," on which he
rested his hopes for fame, is equally a metaphor in such an

age, since the authority for the value of literary productions does not rest in the author's hands alone. Authority is a social nexus, not a personal possession; and if the authority for specific literary works is initiated anew for each new work by some specific artist, its initiation takes place in a necessary and integral historical environment of great complexity. Most immediately—and this is what concerns us here—it takes place within the conventions and enabling limits that are accepted by the prevailing institutions of literary production—conventions and limits which exist for the purpose of generating and supporting literary production. In all periods those institutions adapt to the special needs of individuals, including the needs of authors (some of whom are more comfortable with the institutions than others). But whatever special arrangments are made, the essential fact remains: literary works are not produced without arrangements of some sort.

One final remark on the authority assumed by the institutions of literary production. When we observe literary works from the special and narrowed focus of the textual critic, we tend to think that this issue of authority involves only people like author, amanuensis, publisher, editor, printer. Because of this special focus, textual critics conceive problems like "final intention" in the terms we have been observing, that is, as if the production of literary works—and hence the problem of the authority for various problematical readings—were a struggle between the pen of the author, the pencil of the editor, and the mechanized tools of the printer. But let us reflect for a moment on the case of Tennyson. This was a poet who frequently revised his work on the basis of the responses he received from a small circle of friends (at the trial proof stage) as well as from reviewers and the larger audience (at the publication stage). On whose authority were the changes made in the 1832 *Poems,* or in *The Princess,* or in *Maud?* Clearly, to ask such a question is to misconceive the nature of the problem, for the changes do not spring from a single *fons et origo.*

4. A Modern Instance: Editing Byron

A commonplace idea used to prevail that Byron—in the words of Paul Elmer More—"was perfectly reckless" about the accidentals of his poetry, so that the contemporary published works "represent the taste of Murray's advisers rather than that of the poet."[58] An editor following the Bowers tradition might take this comment as a license to return to Byron's manuscripts for the copy-texts in a critical edition, since these "at least . . . reflect his, rather than someone else's, intentions."[59] Being of a different school, however, More took the following line: "Since the old punctuation did not at all emanate from the poet, . . . no scruple has been felt in altering it as far as was desired." More's decision to modernize is not a fault, since he was not producing a critical edition; nor is that decision my principal interest at the moment. Rather, what strikes one is the peculiar area of agreement between More's position and that of Bowers: both assume that authority in these matters should lie with the author, whether he assumed that authority or not, and whether or not the conditions of authorship even permitted the assumption of such an autonomy. In fact, however, an author's work possesses autonomy only when it remains an unheard melody. As soon as it begins its passage to publication it undergoes a series of interventions which some textual critics see as a process of contamination, but which may equally well be seen as a process of training the poem for its appearances in the world.

This training, or contamination, begins with the author's first revisions and editorial corrections, and it continues through the proof stage, the publication, and the subsequent reprintings both during and after the poet's lifetime. Many persons besides the author are engaged in these events, and the entire process constitutes the life of an important social institution at the center of which is the literary work itself (the "work" being a series of specific "texts," a series of specific acts of production, and the entire process which both of these series constitute). For the textual critic, all phases and aspects of these matters are relevant.[60]

In Byron's case, certain elements in this complex network assume particular importance for the textual critic. Throughout his life Byron sought editorial help with his poetry, so that people like R. C. Dallas, J. C. Hobhouse, Thomas Moore, his publisher John Murray, and Murray's chief editor William Gifford all exerted a significant impact upon Byron's literary work. Perhaps even more interesting is the influence of Mary Shelley on so much of Byron's work written after he left England in 1816.[61] She was one among a number of people who served as Byron's amanuenses at various periods of his life. She was one of the most important ones, however, not merely because she made the press copies for many of Byron's most important works, but also because she sometimes altered Byron's drafts. The changes she introduced into her fair copies were both substantive and accidental, and in the end many of them appeared in the original editions. Byron was of course well aware of her interventions: he sometimes corrected back to his initial readings, he sometimes accepted her readings, and occasionally he produced a new reading altogether.

My interest in these matters is not so much in the final editorial decisions which one would have to make about these different readings, nor even in the reasons for such eventual choices. Rather, I want to draw attention to the structure of the situation which such a procedure reveals. Here certain relations are prevailing between author and copyist which are not purely mechanical. Furthermore, both author and copyist understand and operate within the accepted terms of the relationship: Byron and Mary Shelley continued to work in this way from 1816 until he left Italy for Greece in 1823. Indeed, their relationship is nothing less than a paradigm which operates through all periods of Byron's literary career, and with all persons in his literary world who had a hand in publishing his poetry.

Furthermore, all the historical evidence suggests that this is the structure which normally prevails between authors and the literary institutions within which they operate. From the (mostly) anonymous scribes of the Middle Ages to the famous cases of the twentieth century—Maxwell Perkins, for example, or *The Autobiography of Malcolm X*[62]—authors and their literary agents (or employers) have collaborated to varying degrees in the transmission of literary works. Sometimes these relationships operate smoothly, sometimes the author will struggle against every sort of intervention, and between these two extremes falls every sort of variation. Nevertheless, as soon as a person begins writing for publication, he or she becomes an author, and this means—by (historical) definition—to have entered the world of all those who belong to the literary institution. Blake's decision to seek complete freedom from that institution, though futile, is nonetheless an important limiting case, for it sharply underscores the determining authority of the institution. Indeed, Blake's personal freedom from that social authority has become valuable to us, and to society at large, only when the institution found it possible, after Blake's death, to acquire greater authority over his works, and thereby to save them from oblivion.

When we speak of the working relations which exist between author and publishing institutions, we obviously do not mean to suggest that final authority for literary works rests with institutional persons other than the author. Authors are traditionally protective of their works when they deliver them over to the persons who must publish them. Chaucer's famous injunction to his scribe and the copyright laws have much in common.[63] Such authorial concerns are a necessary function of the set of relations which prevail in literary production. The point to be emphasized, however, is that those relations of production do not sanction a theory of textual criticism based upon the concept of the autonomy of the author. "Final authority" for literary works rests neither with the author nor with his affiliated institution; it resides in the actual structure of the agreements which these two cooperating authorities reach in specific cases.

5. Final Intentions and
Textual Versions

Because of the special historical circumstances under which textual criticism has developed, the crucial problem facing the editor of modern texts has come to involve a determination of final intentions, as we have seen. This problem has to be solved because its solution enables the editor who works under the prevailing rules to decide upon a copy-text for his critical edition. According to the Gaskell-Thorpe line of reasoning, the first edition will normally be chosen as copy-text because it lies closest to "the text as the author wanted it to be read."[64] But the Bowers position is that the author's manuscript is a higher authority—is closer to the author's final intentions—since it does not contain any of the contaminations produced during the work's passage through the press.

These rival positions share the view that the rule of final intentions will govern the choice of copy-text. My argument here is that such decisions need not finally depend upon any concept of author's intentions at all. Greg does not employ such a concept in his rationale at least partly because he understood so well the social and historical circumstances under which Shakespeare's texts were produced. Because the concept of author's intentions does not find a clear and unambiguous purchase in the reality of those productive circumstances, it cannot be used as the ultimate measure for determining editorial decisions.

When editors are dealing with later works, however, decisions about copy-text have increasingly come to involve determinations about authorial intentions. This situation has evolved in response to the received textual materials on the one hand, and on the other to the literary conditions which came to prevail in the more recent periods. This we have already observed. In the recent evolution of the theory of intentions, however, the concept has come to be used not merely as a determinant (and it should only be one among several such determinants in any case) of copy-text, but as a guide to the choice of which version of a text we choose to work from. This guide is invoked for works produced in the later modern periods because of the mass of documentary evidence which frequently presents itself to the critic. But sorting through this material with the aid of a concept like authorial intentions frequently only adds confusion to the analysis. Furthermore, it is a concept whose theoretical assumptions tend to obscure the very nature of the problems an editor has to deal with. The concept can be confusing because it hypothesizes two related phenomena which do not and cannot exist: an autonomous author, and an ideal ("finally intended") text. I have already gone into the problems involved in the concept of the autonomous author. Let me turn now to the second matter.

The idea of a finally intended text corresponds to the "lost original" which the textual critics of classical works sought to reconstruct by recension. Both are "ideal texts"[65]— that is to say, they do not exist in fact—but in each case the critics use this ideal text heuristically, as a focussing device for studying the extant documents. Both classical and modern editors work toward their ideal text by a process of recension that aims to approximate the Ideal as closely as possible. Both are termini ad quem which, though not strictly reachable, enable the critic to isolate and remove accumulated error.

For the critic of modern texts, the classical model upon which his own procedures are based frequently does not suit the materials he is studying, and has often served, in the end, to confuse his procedures. Because this textual critic actually possesses the "lost originals" which the classical critic is forced to hypothesize, his concept of an ideal text reveals itself to be—paradoxically—a pure abstraction, whereas the classical critic's ideal text remains, if "lost," historically actual. Modern editors who possess a large body of prepublication materials therefore stand in an entirely different relation to the editorial situation than do their classical counterparts.

The classical editor's copy-text (in McKerrow's "general sense") is chosen following an analysis of the reconstructed stemma. Copy-text serves the editor as a means of arranging his apparatus and of adjudicating textual cruxes when reason and learning fail. In short, it helps to isolate possible corruptions when the documentation cannot positively decide the issue. But the editor of modern texts does not typically work in the sort of darkness that surrounds the classical editor, or the editors of an author like Langland. In such cases, the problem of textual corruption is of an order of magnitude so vastly different from the problem as it appears in modern texts that it amounts to an entirely different sort of problem.[66] Critics who actually use the classical model for editing modern works, then, set themselves to the wheel of an error-removing process which has no proper application to the documents and circumstances, and which, as a result, tends to obscure from view the special character of their editorial problems. For the editor of late modern works especially, the first and crucial problem is not how to discover corruptions, but how to distinguish and finally choose between textual versions. Stemmatics is a straightforward matter here since the "ancestral series" is relatively unmarked by terrible gaps, obscurities, and ambiguous relations. The wide range of published and prepublished textual forms which the modern editor has at his disposal corresponds to various sorts of "intention" conceived by the author alone, or by the author working in concert with the literary institution of his time and place. Under these conditions, the critical editor is not normally seeking an author's final intentions, since he does not need such an ideal text in the same way and for the same reasons that the editor of classical texts does. On the contrary, the editor of modern texts is typically concerned to distinguish the type and character of actual, achieved, and largely uncorrupted textual forms. Hans Zeller's concept of textual versions is an effort to come to grips with this special fact about modern texts, and to offer a means of marking out the distinctive features of the several versions of a particular work.

A parenthetical remark in Gaskell's discussion of "textual bibliography" calls attention to the same problem.

> It is an anomaly of bibliographical scholarship today that, while much effort is expended on the textual bibliography of nineteenth-century books of which the early texts differ from each other only in minor and frequently trivial ways, books of which we have texts in several widely different forms are either avoided by editors or edited in a single version. This may be because the methods evolved for the textual bibliography of Shakespeare, where minor variation is seldom trivial, can be applied to the first class of book but not to the second.[67]

Gaskell is certainly right when he says that a model from Shakespearean studies has been allowed to obscure some of the central problems in the textual criticism of modern works.

Indeed, fresh advances in the theory of textual criticism have been slow to come because we have failed to grasp the special sorts of problem raised by such works.

Another example from Byron may prove useful. *The Giaour*, as I noted earlier, descends to us in a complex number of prepublication and published forms. In this respect it is typical of the extant documentation for Byron's earlier works. The most important of these are the holograph draft (344 lines), the fair copy (375 lines), the trial proof (453 lines), the first edition (684 lines), second edition (816 lines), third edition, first issue (950 lines) and second issue (1,014 lines), fourth edition (1,048 lines), fifth edition (1,215 lines), and seventh edition (1,334 lines). Among these early published texts Byron corrected press for the first, third, fifth, and seventh editions. The work passed through fourteen editions between 1813 and 1815, and the system of accidentals established in the first edition was completely overhauled in the third, fifth, seventh, and thirteenth editions.

According to received theory (and Gaskell agrees with Bowers in this matter), copy-text will be decided on a judgment about Byron's final intentions toward his work's accidentals. But the facts plainly demonstrate that the very concept of final intentions has only a minor relevance in this situation. One might argue that an eclectic text should be constructed on the basis of the first edition, with the later additions and revisions incorporated from the subsequent editions or manuscripts. But the result of such a process would be a text marked throughout by "accidental" distractions—variations in styles of punctuation and capitalization which result from different and competing accidental systems (the early editions tend to a rhetorical style of punctuation, where the later grow increasingly syntactical and tightly organized).

The purely textual facts in this case conceal—or rather encode— the story of a complex set of developing relationships between Byron, John Murray and his publishing agents, and Byron's readers of 1812-15. Threading through the story are various arbitrary elements and events, some of which we know a great deal about, some of which we do not. Various typesetters were used to set the poem and its many additions, and various people proofed it at different times. The poem's readers and reviewers were another important influence upon the work's development and process of accretion. For that matter, why Byron ceased adding new passages to the poem after the seventh edition is by no means apparent, anymore than we can now see clearly why Byron did not proof the second or the fourth (or even the thirteenth) edition when he took the trouble about the others. Furthermore, while the extant documentation for this work is massive, we do not know how carefully Byron proofed the later editions, although it *is* clear that he proofed more than simply the new additions to each of the new printings.

In general, the poem's early composition, publication, and reception histories testify to the development of a work whose accidentals, and sometimes even whose substantives, were introduced into the work by a poet unusually responsive to his immediate literary environment. From the outset Byron accepts the general terms of the publishing institution of his day— that is, the division of labor against which Blake had been so vigorously revolting. Beyond this, he maintains and he delegates authority, gives it away (willingly or passively), and sometimes reassumes it again, in whole or in part. Byron of course always remains the poem's "author," but the critical concept of textual authority is not one which can be easily superimposed upon his autonomous historical self. Furthermore, the critical concepts of authorial intentions and final intentions lose their precision and neat applicability under the conditions which I have been summarizing. Several sorts of purpose and intention impinge on the poem, and Byron's textual intentions occasionally disappear under the pressure of other people's. As regards the poem's substance, "final intentions" seems to be a relatively determinate matter (it is not always so), but as regards the poem's accidentals one can reasonably doubt that Byron ever had any final intentions, or whether his intentions were determinate at any point in the process of the poem's production.[68] In a case of this kind, Greg is a better guide to an editorial practice than is Bowers.

The situation illustrates what Zeller had in mind when he spoke of works existing in different versions. Although I have presented *The Giaour* as an example of a problem in copy-text rather than a problem of versions, the *structure of the situation* which generates the editorial problem is the same as that which Zeller has called attention to. His proposal is that the editor must analyze textual variations not in an atomic and seriatim fashion, but systemically, since each work—each text of a work—"consists not of its elements but of the relationships between them."[69] Such relationships appear to the critic as purely textual formations, whereas in fact the textual relationships are only the signs of others, and will be understood only in terms of those underlying relationships. When texts are "established" in the process of literary production, they typically emerge not in simple ancestral series, but in lateral divergence patterns. As these various texts are descriptively distinguished, the critic's task will not normally be to choose version and copy-text on the basis of final intentions. In making his judgment the critic will obviously take authorial intentions into account, but only because those intentions help to illuminate the contours of the generic structural patterns and relationshps which define the several constitutions of a particular work. The received textual forms reflect the achieved results of an actual literary production; typically, the forms represent divergent patterns of varying purposes and intentions rather than an ancestral series in which we are trying to track down the author's final intentions.

Were we dealing with psychological rather than social phenomena, we could properly say that the forms reflect authorial intentions. But a textual history is a psychic history only because it is first a social history. This is not a metaphysical fact about literary works, but one which is functionally related to and determined by the purposes of literary works, on the one hand, and the programs which seek to study them on the other. The stories one may extract from a textual history are sometimes psychological stories, as we may particularly observe in the case of authorial manuscripts. But even there, especially in the fair copy manuscripts, the stories reflect social interactions and purposes, and as soon as we begin to study the proofs and the editions the psychological focus begins to recede into a subplot. We enter the world of textual versions where intentions are plainly shifting and changing under the pressure of various people and circumstances.

The early textual history of *The Giaour*, as outlined above, does not tell a story of textual contamination then. Of course, textual contaminations occur frequently throughout that early productive process, and another history would be able to tell the story of such contaminations. But the history as given above is primarily a schematic outline of the factors affecting the development of the earliest versions of *The Giaour*. It reveals the systematic transformation which all literary works undergo in their production. Those transformations—what I have called above the "achieved results" of an actual productive process—involve the translation of an initially psychological phenomenon (the "creative process") into a social one (the literary work).

6

Final Authorial Intentions: Exceptions and Misconceptions

These examples force us to inquire further into the related concepts of authorial intentions and authorship itself. Such ideas seem transparent and elementary, but in fact they conceal a network of conceptual ambiguities which necessarily result in procedural difficulties of various kinds. Before we take these problems up, let me recapitulate some relevant matters.

The rule of final intentions is an editorial construct which has a particular and explicable development in the history of scholarship. It evolved out of circumstances which initially defined a concept of "author's intentions" or "author's original intentions," but which subsequently yielded to the formulation "author's final intentions." This conclusive form of the rule emerged when textual critics began to study works produced in the later modern periods, where large masses of prepublication materials have to be dealt with. It is, furthermore, a concept which emerges through the Lachmann-Greg tradition, that is to say, through a tradition which conceives that the study of texts must be carried out within the terms defined by an ancestral series. In this situation, the critic seeks to arrange his texts in order to sort out the least corrupt line of textual descent. Joseph Bédier's critique of this approach is interesting and important because his study of medieval texts led him to very different conclusions about textual recension and emendation procedures. In Bédier's view, to seek a reconstruction of some original work from later textual constitutions was often both impossible and misguided. The best procedure, in such circumstances, would be to seek after the "best text" among the extant documents and edit that.[70]

Plainly, such an approach has set aside altogether any concept of authorial intentions. One does not try to reconstitute a lost original document—this is the heroic task which Kane and Donaldson have set for themselves—nor does one seek to produce an eclectic text based upon a hypothesized intention in the author. As different and even as antithetical as these two approaches are, both accept the Lachmann premise of ancestral series and both seek to recover some form of original and authorial text. So, although Greg does not activate a concept of authorial intentions in his theory of copy-text, the form of his thought—in contrast to the form of Bédier's—leaves itself open to an intentionalistic interpretation. It was Bowers, as we have seen, who introduced such an interpretation. The concept of final authorial intentions is therefore functionally related to the theory of the copy-text.

Eugene Vinaver's great edition of Malory, which I shall discuss more particularly below, offers an interesting example of a work which stands, from the point of view of theory, half way between Bédier and Lachmann. Vinaver's edition explicitly invokes Bédier when he speaks of the "base" manuscript which "has been adopted for this edition," but he reveals other critical allegiances just as clearly when he observes of textual criticism in general: "The primary aim of any critical edition is a text which would approach as closely as the extant material allows to the original form of the work."[71] In editing Malory and similar texts, the concepts of copy-text and final authorial intentions simply have no ready application. Nevertheless, Vinaver's work is produced under the influence of Lachmann's stemmatic quest for the lost original.

Critical concepts of authorial intentions begin to appear when certain historical circumstances come to prevail in the discipline—specifically, when textual critics trained in the same traditions which nurtured Bédier and Vinaver turn their attention to works of the more modern periods. Large masses of monogenously related textual materials called for systematic procedures which would facilitate analysis, in the way that Lachmann's procedures had facilitated the analysis of polygenous texts. As textual critics developed their methods for sorting out the final intentions from these masses of editorial and textual data, the very rule of final intentions began to be placed in a critical position. This we have already observed, in a general way, in the various exceptions and problematic cases which editors and critics have raised against the rule from time to time. Of course, the rule has never been easily applied to classical works, the Bible, or to texts produced in earlier periods—to Chaucer's or to Langland's texts, for example, or even to Shakespeare's. But since the rule was developed to deal principally with works from the later modern periods, these special deviations have not seemed crucial. Nevertheless, numerous problematic cases continue to be instanced from eighteenth- to twentieth-century texts, and these have begun to place the rule of final authorial intentions under considerable pressure. The argument-by-exception has thus far brought about the collapse of the idea of the "definitive edition,"[72] a change in critical thinking which signals the crisis now facing the Bowers line. The fact that Tanselle has been called upon to write a series of lengthy defenses of the line is a further symptom of the crisis.

My argument here is that the problem cases raised by various commentators are not properly understood as exceptions to a "normal" editorial situation, but as signs that the textual-critical theories which dominate our approaches to

early-modern and modern works have failed to define properly either (a) the status and nature of "the text," or (b) the
correspondent obligations which the critical editor has toward
his work. My view is that editors cannot follow the guidance
of a rule of final authorial intentions in determining the texts
they will print because final authorial intention is a deeply
problematic concept. Though this is evidently the case in relation to works produced in very early periods, the concept is
especially treacherous in relation to more recent works
because it seems so clear and simple at the level of theory and
method.

Practical problems, particular cases, reveal the ambiguity
in the concept, and I want to begin here to generalize those
particular case problems. Only then will we be able to see
that we are not dealing with exceptional instances but with a
structural fault in the very concept of final intentions as it has
been used and understood. Let me say here, however, that we
are interested in cases where the rule of final intentions cannot, does not, or will not apply, not in order to destroy this
important tool of textual criticism, but in order to clarify the
range and field of its usefulness.

I will begin with two patterns of texts—or classes of textual problems—which we may observe to short-circuit the
easy operation of the rule of final intentions. The first of these
involves cases where we cannot determine final authorial
intentions because we have multiple versions, all of which
exert equivalent claims upon the editor. Zeller instances
famous examples like *The Prelude*, but this class is an
extremely diverse one embracing a wide range of authors and
types of work. Editors have always been aware of this sort of
problem, and the facing-page resolution has been the normal
method of accommodation. Such an accommodation is in
fact perfectly adequate so long as it does not obscure for us

the conceptual problem which this rule of accommodation has evaded.

The problem is restored to view when we look at a few extreme cases from this class of texts—cases, that is to say, which will not easily submit to a facing-page solution. The enormous mass of so-called occasional poems would supply any number of examples. Byron's "Windsor Poetics" is a good example.[73] The number of versions of this epigram nearly correspond to the number of extant copies, of which there are many. The character of the piece explains the editorial problems it raises. A political poem ridiculing the Prince Regent and monarchal authority in general, the poem was not written for publication, but for private circulation in manuscript form, chiefly among Byron's friends and the Whig circles of his period. Byron himself gave copies to several friends and acquaintances who shared his political views, and he expected that the epigram would be more widely disseminated as further copies were made from the originals and from the secondary copies as well. Byron is directly responsible for at least three versions, but the work is of such a character that it can hardly be said to lie under his sole authority in any case. The poem exists in a state analogous to (though not identical with) the state in which traditional ballads descend to us.

Byron wrote many occasional poems of this sort—works which he either could not or would not publish in his lifetime, and some of which he never wanted published at all. In this respect his practice is typical, and Landor's works provide numerous similar instances. Landor would typically send a poem to (say) Lady Blessington in a letter, and he might later publish a more formal version—sometimes more than one formal version. But Landor's works are notorious not so much for this sort of textual situation as for another one which reveals a different type of textual multiplication. That is to say, Landor frequently wrote verses which he then reworked in various ways to accommodate them to different circumstances and publications.

I do not have in mind here Landor's perpetual habit of tinkering with his texts, or of introducing changes as the works moved through subsequent publications in his lifetime. These cases are famous and they include "Ianthe" ("Past ruin'd Ilion") as well as "To Ianthe (In Vienna)." In the former poem Landor dropped the final stanza from the initial printed version, and in the latter he omitted the first ten lines when he reprinted. These are interesting cases because readers generally find that the first poem benefits from the excision of the final stanza, whereas the loss of the first ten lines in the other seems a much less certain benefit.

Difficult as such poems are when later editors have to make decisions about the reading text, they will submit to a Bowers line of interpretation, though it remains a moot question whether such a line ought to be followed. In any case, the problems are simple when compared with another set of typical Landor works. Like many other poets, Landor often took verses which he first wrote or published in one form or another and used them later in entirely different circumstances. Joseph Warren Beach has pointed to Auden's frequent resort to this practice (see below, pp. 87-89), and we see it in Landor as well. The *Imaginary Conversations* contain numerous instances of verses which were later reprinted as separate poems incorporating integral titles and textual changes of various kinds. Thus, the poem "Sophocles to Poseidon," published in the 1847 *Hellenics*, initially appeared in 1824 as part of the "Pericles and Sophocles" *Imaginary Conversation*, and the same is true of "Regeneration" and numerous other verses by Landor. (One has difficulty calling them "poems" or "works" since they seem such adaptable and shape-shifting creatures.)

Far from an exceptional pattern of behavior, Landor's practice here is typical of many poets' work. The charming lyric commonly known as "To Ianthe" ("A voice I heard and hear it yet") offers a peculiarly interesting case of Landor's manipulation of his texts and—as a consequence—of subsequent editorial difficulties. Landor's manuscript poem is titled "To Ianthe" and runs as follows:

> A voice I heard and hear it yet,
> "We meet not so again,
> My silly tears you must forget
> Or they may give you pain."
>
> The tears that on two faces meet
> My Muse forbids to dry,
> She keeps them ever fresh and sweet
> When hours and years run by.
>
> She bids me send this verse to you . . .
> "Go tell him still to be
> (Without a tear) as fond and true
> And leave the rest to me."

When Landor came to print these verses in *Heroic Idyls* (1863), however, they appeared without a title and as two separate poems entirely. The first was printed thus on page 213:

> A VOICE I heard and hear it yet,
> We meet not so again;
> My silly tears you must forget,
> Or they may give you pain.

This epigram was then followed by two brief pieces, one titled "Calverton Downs" and the second "On Some Obscure Poetry." Then came another untitled epigram which turned out to be the second stanza of the original manuscript work. And that was that. Lines 9-12 from the manuscript poem were never printed by Landor.

A further change was made in this poem by Stephen Wheeler when he came to print it in his great edition.[74] Wheeler printed stanzas 1-2 as a single integral poem under the title "To Ianthe" and he placed lines 9-12 in an apparatus note. That is to say, Wheeler created a poem which Landor seems never to have put together at any time (it is, however, a very good poem in its own right). Wheeler went on to say that "In 1863 two other epigrams are wrongly printed between stanzas i-ii, which are here brought together as in the author's manuscript." Thus was produced the eight-line version of this lyric, nor did Wheeler at all think he was creating something Landor never "intended". On the contrary, Wheeler certainly felt that the eight-line poem *was* what Landor intended.

We reach this last conclusion because (a) Wheeler was a shrewd and scrupulous editor, and (b) the extant manuscript, along with the circumstances surrounding the publication of *Heroic Idyls*, led Wheeler to this conviction. The book was the last published in Landor's lifetime, and it was put together in the most confusing and disordered set of circumstances. Landor was always a difficult author for a publisher to work with since he was simultaneously volatile, arbitrary, and meticulous, especially about his poetry. He tinkered with his texts repeatedly and placed extraordinary demands upon his printers and publishers. But the editing of *Heroic Idyls* took place when Landor's already difficult temperament was exacerbated by increasing senility and loss of memory. The story is well known and has been splendidly

told by R. H. Super in *The Publication of Landor's Works*.[75]
Under these circumstances, Wheeler looked at the twelve-line
manuscript text and then at the two separated four-line epigrams in the book, and he concluded, not unreasonably, that
the fiasco of the book's printing history resulted in a mistake.
In Wheeler's judgment, Landor's final intention was to print
a single eight-line epigram in *Heroic Idyls*, not the twelve-line
epigram and not two separate four-line epigrams.

Wheeler's version of the poem may be what Landor
wanted, but then again it may not be. Furthermore, what
Landor wanted might well be considered a secondary consideration under the circumstances. Three options are available to a later editor, and the evidence we have could be used
to justify the choice of any one of the three.

Heroic Idyls contains a fair number of other works which
illustrate similar problems in defining final intentions. "A
Mother to a Boy" appears in two different versions in the
book (165, 217) and so do "The Later Day" and "The Former
Day" (216, 196), as well as the verses beginning "We hear no
more an attic song" (197, 267). The poem "Eucrates to the
God Sleep" (79) and "An Old Poet to Sleep" (123) are
different versions of the same work. Of course, these double
versions were printed in *Heroic Idyls* only because of special
local circumstances. They are important in the context of this
discussion, however, not primarily because they present problems of choice between different versions, but because they
underscore a widespread practice among poets. If *Heroic Idyls*
represents an exceptional case among Landor's books, its
peculiar difficulties only exist for the editor because of
Landor's habit of using his texts to generate various sorts of
literary work. Eclectic reconstruction of an "authoritative"
text—a standard operation in contemporary editorial
procedure—is not appropriate here.

These examples lead us to suspect that the general criterion of author's intentions in its current acceptation—that is, as the conceptual ideal which guides our editorial practice—may be leading textual critics astray by obscuring the true character of literary production. A second group of texts enforces this suspicion—somewhat paradoxically, in fact, for this group includes works whose process of socialization has been partially arrested.

This class of texts includes those for which the author never brought his work to a point where an editor can speak of final intentions at all. Once again we are not dealing with a relatively circumscribed set of texts. This class includes some of the most celebrated works in our heritage, and it possibly comprises—in sheer numbers of textual items—nearly as large a corpus as what we have of fully "authorized" and published works. To supply many examples is unnecessary; one need only mention Shelley's "The Triumph of Life" to organize this class for our attention.

An important paradox emerges when we come to deal with these sorts of text, as the following demonstration will show. In treating them critically we begin by focusing almost wholly on the author and the relative state of completion which his work shows. Furthermore, to edit such works means that we deal with them in their early (document) state. These circumstances force us to choose a textual version which conforms to the Bowers rule (i.e., an authorial manuscript, if available). But note that this conformity is purely accidental, and that the rule has in fact no applicability for criticism at all. We have only one authorial manuscript to "choose from" when preparing a critical edition of "The Triumph of Life" or "The Fall of Hyperion." Editorial emendation, of course, is not yet an issue, and hence the problem of copy-text remains to this point as irrelevant as the rule of final intentions.

If, on the other hand, uncompleted works descend to us in several authorial manuscript versions, the critic must establish procedures for distinguishing such texts in order to make choices between them. I propose that we speak of early, medial, and late manuscript versions. These distinctions do not correspond to draft, corrected draft, and fair copy texts, since these latter traditional terms serve to elucidate part of the monogenous stemma, and hence presuppose the concept of completed intentions. They are important concepts, but they confuse the issue when the contemporary textual situation is restricted to pre-publication forms. Under conditions where the author's publishing institutions are not involved in the production of the work, the author's fair copy does not necessarily represent the author's final intentions but only the latest manuscript state of the work. As yet the editorial concept of intentions—even were we inclined, following Bowers, to invoke it—would have no operational application.

At this point we should be able to see the theoretical importance of these texts for criticism. They are peculiarly significant because they reveal the paradox implicit in the concept of authorial intention. In their earliest "completed" forms these texts remain more or less wholly under the author's control, yet as a class they are texts for which the editorial concept of intention has no meaning. These texts show, in other words, that the concept of authorial intention only comes into force for criticism when (paradoxically) the artist's work begins to engage with social structures and functions. The fully authoritative text is therefore always one which has been socially produced; as a result, the critical standard for what constitutes authoritativeness cannot rest with the author and his intentions alone.

Once again let me have recourse to Byron to illustrate these matters. I have in mind the cases of major works like "To the Po" and the "Stanzas" ("Could love for ever"), though many of Byron's posthumously published works would do as well to illustrate my point. I shall here offer only the single example of "To the Po."

First, let me narrate the relevant textual information. Byron's "draft" manuscript (*MS. Mo*) was written on 1 or 2 June 1819. He did not make a revised copy (*MS. B*) until 14 April 1820, at which time he sent *MS. B* to his friend Douglas Kinnaird in a letter. There are no other holograph copies of the poem, but at least four transcripts were made of which three survive. All of these ultimately derive from *MS. Mo*.

MS. P is a transcript made by Mary Shelley. It is a careful copy of *MS. Mo* and was almost certainly executed at Albaro late in 1822, when she was copying a number of Byron's manuscripts for him. *MSS. P* and *Mo* were among the manuscripts which he left with Teresa Guiccioli in 1823 when he left Italy for Greece.

MS. A is another transcript made by Mary Shelley; it appears at the end of one of her journal books whose last dated entry (before this transcript) is 4 June 1819. *MS. A* seems to be a copy which she made from *MS. Mo*, but hastily and without the care she took in making *MS. P*.

MS. G is Teresa Guiccioli's transcript made from *MS. P*. *MS. G* was probably executed sometime during 1827-29, as we see from Teresa's correspondence with Mary Shelley and Thomas Moore during that time. On 10 August 1827 she wrote to Mary Shelley saying that she would send Moore transcripts of Byron's unedited poems, and Moore wrote later—29 October 1829—to thank her for the materials she had sent.

Finally, Thomas Medwin must have made a transcript of the poem, but his does not survive. The collation indicates that this transcript—and hence the printed text which was made from it—was probably made from *MS. A* rather than directly from *MS. Mo*.

Byron himself originally thought to publish this famous lyric from *MS. B* in 1821 or 1822, but he finally decided not to. The poem was first printed by Medwin in his *Journal of the Conversations of Lord Byron* (1824). Medwin's text is a problematic one. In the first place, it derives from *MS. Mo* rather than from *MS. B*; in the second place, its descent from *MS. Mo* seems to be through *MS. A*, the worst of the intermediate transcripts; finally, and most seriously, Medwin's text introduced a number of readings which do not appear in Byron's own surviving manuscripts.

The poem was next printed in the collected edition of 1831 which used the Medwin printed version as copy-text but which resorted to *MS. G* for corroboration of its readings in certain cases. Also, the 1831 edition introduced a few of its own alterations into its base text from Medwin. The 1831 text was copy text for the first standard collected edition of 1832-33; all subsequent printings descend from these last two.

Thus one can see that all currently available printed texts of the poem seem to be based on Byron's draft manuscript, not on the revised copy which he had once thought to print. Furthermore, because all printed texts can be traced back to Medwin as their most important immediate source, all currently available texts provide the reader with Medwin's version of the poem, which differs considerably from both holograph manuscripts.

This is a complicated history which raises many more textual issues than I can comment upon here. What I want to emphasize is the character of the nonauthorial copies made directly or indirectly from *MS. Mo*, for it is these copies which help to elucidate the textual status of Byron's holographs. *Mo* is an early—indeed, a draft—manuscript, whereas *B* is a later one, a corrected copy made from *Mo*. But we would do well here to speak of these as early and later manuscripts rather than as drafts and corrected copies because Byron's editorial intentions toward the poem are not a precisely determinable matter. That we cannot speak of *B* as representing Byron's final or even latest intentions is patent. Mary Shelley's first copy, *MS. P*, emphasizes the crucial fact that Byron seems not to have regarded *Mo* as a superseded or corrupt or inaccurate text. Medwin's printed version raises the further possibility that Byron made another copy of his poem based on *Mo* which differed from *B* and which conformed more closely to what Medwin printed. We do not know. But even were we to hypothesize this as a fact, the methodological issue remains the same. In such a case we would simply have two "later" manuscripts rather than one. What we would still not have would be either the warrant or the opportunity to invoke the editorial concept of author's final intentions to decide the practical choices we should have to make when editing the poem. That concept only becomes available when an author enters into publishing arrangements.   In this case, Byron died before such arrangements were set in motion, and the consequence is that his intentions cannot be appealed to for final textual determinations.

   This class of texts—where final intentions were never achieved and hence where the editorial category of intentions is itself rendered extremely problematic—is so large and complex that critics will have eventually to analyze its special characteristics and forms. Recently we have been reminded of this sort of text through the rather acrimonious re-emergence of the problem of Thomas Wolfe's works, and especially of the last three novels published under his name and from his unfinished corpus of literary remains.[76] That these were editorially reconstructed has long been known, as we have also known Maxwell Perkins's extensive collaborative involvement in the making of Wolfe's first three novels. This early productive history is important for understanding the posthumous situation, for it shows the productive method which Wolfe finally settled upon: that is to say, it shows his dependence upon the editorial assistance of his publishing house.

Consequently, the mere existence of an unpublished Wolfe manuscript, whether apparently "finished" or not, cannot be approached the way one would approach an unpublished manuscript by Keats or Browning. In Wolfe's case, the question of author's intentions will always remain problematic. As far as the three posthumous novels are concerned, their editorial reconstruction—chiefly by Edward Aswell, of Harper and Row, but with the assistance of Perkins and Elizabeth Nowell—is precisely what we would expect to find if Wolfe's literary remains were to be published as novels at all. Printing Wolfe's posthumous manuscripts in the form in which he left them would be to print an extended excerpt from the case history of a writer-at-work, and an eccentric writer at that. It would not be printing a novel in any sense, however interesting the documents might be for other reasons. Besides, such a project—given Wolfe's history as a publishing writer—would mean engaging in another sort of editorial reconstruction, paradoxical as that may seem. It might prove an interesting publishing project were anyone to undertake such a venture. It would certainly present Wolfe's work in a light that never was on land or sea.

Important writers always leave unpublished work behind them. These situations, perhaps more than any others, provide dramatic evidence of the fact that all writers always work under an imperative of "collaboration." Swinburne left at his death one of his most impressive works, the early uncompleted novel we now call *Lesbia Brandon*. Unlike Wolfe, Swinburne was a meticulous craftsman, but the fragments of this prose work seem to have been left in a relatively inchoate state. Swinburne seems not to have been able to choose between several structural options, so that we are left with a number of relatively complete units whose interrelations are not always precisely determinable. The brilliance of these pieces is such, however, that they were posthumously edited and published by Randolph Hughes.[77] The relative adequacy of Hughes's reconstruction has been questioned, and *Lesbia Brandon* will certainly be edited again, perhaps with better results. Whatever the case, *Lesbia Brandon* will never appear in a form which the author finally intended. Indeed, part of the enduring charm of the work lies in its unfinished character.

7

The Problem
of Literary Authority

These two groups of problematic cases expose, it seems to me, the fundamental nature of the issues which must be faced. The rule of final authorial intentions, as well as the guidelines determining choice of copy-text, all rest on an assumption about the location (and the locatability) of literary authority. As the very term "authority" suggests, the author is taken to be—for editorial and critical purposes—the ultimate locus of a text's authority, and literary works are consequently viewed in the most personal and individual way. Furthermore, just as literary works are narrowly identified with an author, the identity of the author with respect to the work is critically simplified through this process of individualization. The result is that the dynamic social relations which always exist in literary production—the dialectic between the historically located individual author and the historically developing institutions of literary production—tends to become obscured in criticism. Authors lose their lives as they gain such critical identities, and their works suffer a similar fate by being divorced from the social relationships which gave them their lives (including their "textual" lives) in the first place, and which sustain them through their future life in society.

This set of issues needs to be examined closely, and I want to begin with the case of Malory's *Morte d'Arthur*. This work's chief line of descent into the twentieth century is through the text printed by William Caxton. But in the early part of this century the Winchester Manuscript of the work was discovered, and the evidence provided in this new text—principally in the now famous colophon at the end of book 4—suggested that the Winchester text stood in a closer relation to Malory than did Caxton's printed version. Eugene Vinaver eventually produced an edition of Malory based on the Winchester Manuscript, and his presentation of the text there emphasized, quite correctly, the authorial connection. Although Vinaver was too scrupulous a scholar to argue that the Winchester text was more authoritative than Caxton's, he continually pushed the reader toward such a conclusion. We see this clearly in his following general comment on the relative difference between Caxton's text and the Winchester Manuscript. "The Winchester scribes copy their text mechanically and seldom, if ever, attempt to correct it. Caxton, on the other hand, is an editor rather than a scribe."[78]

This sort of remark betrays Vinaver's predilection to believe that a text which shows no editorial intervention will be prima facie more sincere than one that exhibits intervention. The scribal text seems less corrupted than Caxton's, and therefore will also seem closer to Malory. This predilection is deeply imbedded in our textual criticism, as we have seen, and in its latest form it serves to validate the theory of copy-text and the rule of final intentions.

Vinaver, however, is aware of the pitfalls which such a predilection can lead an editor into because Vinaver was trained as a scholar of polygenous texts. So when we examine Vinaver's edition we see that its argument for choosing the Winchester Manuscript as base text is rather broadly grounded:

The Winchester MS has been adopted for the present

edition . . . not because it is in every respect nearest to the original, but because it is so in some parts, and because as long as absolute "truthfulness" is not aimed at, the less well known of the two versions, which is at least as reliable as the other, is as fair as any choice can be.[79]

This is unexceptionably expressed. Vinaver's choice of his base text is founded on a shrewd assessment of its distinctive qualities. The Winchester Manuscript differs in sharp and important ways from Caxton's text—principally, it is less ordered and integral in its parts—so that the Winchester version exerts its own strong claim to be printed on its textual merits alone. The colophon which seems to link the manuscript to Malory is important, of course, but hardly regulative or determining. Did it not exist at all Vinaver's edition would remain a powerful and important piece of work. The existence of the colophon did not determine Vinaver's choice of text, it provided Vinaver with a further reason to be interested in the manuscript, on the one hand, and on the other, with a scholar's fact which would be certain to command attention.

Vinaver's edition enters its field, then, not by supplanting the Caxton text with one that is more "authoritative" (least of all "definitive"), but by supplementing it with a new version. Caxton's version has received the sanction of its own history and tradition quite beyond the possibility of abrogation. This is the case, moreover, not merely by accident or force of circumstance, but because Caxton's version exerts various sorts of claim on our attention and respect. That Vinaver is aware of this is clear from his introduction to his edition of the Winchester Manuscript text; that he would like to believe he might be able to discover, or recover, an authorial text wholly uncorrupted by other, intervening authorities is, however, equally clear. The colophon to book 4 focuses the nostalgic attachment which textual criticism has always had for original authorial documents. It has been a functional and important nostalgia, particularly in the work of the early critics of ancient texts and authors. For scholars of more recent periods, however, it is just as likely to operate as a source of confusion.

Vinaver's edition appeals to our longing to read texts which come as clearly and directly from the author's hand as possible. His critical scrupulousness, however, reminds us of the special authority which Caxton's editorially mediated text will always possess. In this way, paradoxically, Vinaver's edition shows that for an editor and textual critic the concept of authority has to be conceived in a more broadly social and cultural context. Authoritative texts are arrived at by an exhaustive reconstruction not of an author and his intentions so much as of an author and his context of work. Even in those cases where the rule of authorial intentions seems determining or even regulative, we must see that it will have been so only *in the event*, that is to say, only after the editor has weighed a great many other factors which bear upon his understanding of the received texts. In cultural products like literary works the location of authority necessarily becomes dispersed beyond the author. When, therefore, Vinaver speaks of "the aim of any critical edition" being to approach as closely as possible the author's original work, he assumes an editorial concept of poetic authority which cannot really be maintained through an analysis.

Textual authority undergoes dispersal and alteration from a number of directions. Bulwer-Lytton's novel *Pelham* illustrates a series of revisions which the author himself took responsibility for as the book moved through its early editions.[80] Which of these texts is the most authoritative however, cannot be decided on Bulwer-Lytton's authority alone. Certain of the revisions seem defensible or even necessary, but many can hardly be judged as other than ruinous and misconceived. Bulwer-Lytton introduced them in response to pressures brought by some of his early readers and reviewers, so that, if later readers and critics see the matter differently, one must judge that the question of authority has not been settled. The editor and textual critic is himself implicated in the determination of that authority. "Under which king, Bezonian—speak, or die."

Sometimes the authority is dispersed among multiple authors. John Ashbery and James Schuyler wrote the novel *A Nest of Ninnies* (1969) together, a peculiar situation which raises interesting questions for the critic. Less peculiar is the similar case of works which are ghost written. I have already mentioned *The Autobiography of Malcolm X* in passing, and one can cite numerous other works of a similar sort, like *Soul on Ice*. Such books are often important pieces of literature rather than ephemeral productions which appeal only to a passing market interest. The problems which these sorts of work locate are not at all dissimilar to those which the earliest modern scholars of the Bible and Homer encountered: when printed material is, in its initial formations, an oral event or testimony, how does one deal with the authority of the text?

Great eighteenth-century scholars opened up these issues, which established the terms in which modern textual criticism could be carried out. Similar problems reappear continually, in new forms of course, and *The Autobiography of Malcolm X* is an especially interesting case because of the reappearance of a nonscriptural level of authority. An editor who came to deal with this work might be tempted to say, simply, that Alex Haley is the principal authority for the "words" while Malcolm X is the authority for the material and "ideas."

Needless to say, it does not require much imagination to realize the problems which would await an approach based upon such distinctions.

Examples like these highlight the problem of the nature of the critical concept of literary authority, but other sorts of case are more useful for expressing the issues at more practical levels. One wishes to consider here notorious examples like Marianne Moore's final intentions toward her poem "Poetry." The three-line version of this work most emphatically represents the author's final intentions toward a poem which she originally published in thirty lines. Nevertheless, it is equally clear that the earlier and longer work will never be superseded by the later revision; indeed, the peculiar force of the revised version depends in important ways upon our knowledge and recollection of the earlier. When we read the following in the 1967 *Complete Poems*:

> I, too, dislike it.
>> Reading it, however, with a perfect contempt for it,
>>> one discovers in
>> it, after all, a place for the genuine.

we probably recall what we saw in the 1935 *Selected Poems*, or in the 1951 *Collected Poems*. Moore's revision is in fact deeply self-conscious about itself and quite a typical example of Moore's genius for low-keyed shock tactics. The three-line version of "Poetry" is a piece of trenchant poetical wit illustrating her concept of stylistic economy and a severe habit of self-discipline. We should probably do well to regard it as a new and separate poem rather than as a revision of the earlier work, and hence to print both—the one following the other—in an edition. Such a decision would, however, depart from Moore's own explicit intentions: she removed the thirty-line "Poetry" from the corpus when she came to put together the *Complete Poems.*

Moore's latest work shows other marks of revision at which readers may justifiably find reason to demur. In "The Steeple-Jack," for example, a long passage has been added to the middle of the poem in the *Complete Poems* text. One could easily follow a Moore line of reasoning to support a retreat to the earlier, more severe text, and the same could be said of poems like "Peter" and "Picking and Choosing." In these cases Moore's revised texts smooth out the odd and striking arrangement of the verse lines in her originals. Once again we have a case of explicit final intentions, but once again we may find good reasons to hesitate before following those intentions.

W. H. Auden's habits of composition and revision present similar problems of authorization. Like Landor, Auden often plundered his earlier work for later and very different textual uses. He was particularly attentive to the opportunities which bibliographical context presented. After 1939 he would often place poems in entirely novel contexts and thereby generate different networks of meaning. In many cases the verbal surface would not be altered in any significant way, but the import would shift dramatically because of the contextual change. The most notorious such case is, I suppose, his prose piece "Depravity: A Sermon" which in its original context in *The Dog Beneath the Skin* (1935) is a highly ironical antireligious parody, but which in its reappearance in the 1945 *Collected Poetry* is so placed that one is forced to read it as a serious religious tract. A similar sort of thing happens in Auden's "Letter to a Wound" when it moves from its original context in *The Orators* (1932) to its final resting place in the *Collected Poetry.*

Situations of these kinds occur frequently in the Auden corpus, and they present serious editorial problems. Joseph Warren Beach, who approached Auden's texts with the eye and interests of an interpreter rather than an editor, saw in them "the hazards a poet runs in putting old wine into new bottles."[81] But in such cases the poet's hazards are as nothing compared to the later editor's, for whereas Auden as writer is free to make and remake his works as he chooses, the editor is obliged to pass on what was done. When Auden's intentions shift and change dramatically, and when the changes take the peculiar contextual forms we see in Auden and Landor, an editor must struggle with problems that the author does not have. Auden's canon must be especially maddening for an editor who follows a Bowers line in seeking to establish a canon of eclectic texts.

We are ordinarily forced to an awareness of such cruxes only when they have to do with important works. Auden's "September 1, 1939" is, like Moore's "Poetry," a famous instance where the issue of authorization descends to us in a problematic state. Auden's final wish was to suppress the poem altogether, and his editor Edward Mendelson has followed that wish in the posthumous *Collected Poems* (1976).[82] The poem itself exists in two optional versions, one without the eighth (the original penultimate stanza). The longer work (of nine stanzas) was first published in the *New Republic* in 1939 and again in the volume *Another Time* (1940). He revised the poem and removed the eighth stanza when he placed it in the 1945 *Collected Poems*.

All the instruments agree that this is one of Auden's most important works, so that a collected edition without it—particularly a posthumous edition—seems an anomaly. Agreement is also general that the removal of the eighth stanza weakens the poem. In all respects, then, the case illustrates the relative nature of authority in matters dealing with cultural products like poems. The author's wishes and intentions are obviously matters of importance, but they must be adverted to and assessed by the textual critic in a more generous social context. As Auden himself once said, poetry "survives/ In the valley of its saying," which is a place where author's wishes, the physical texts, and a host of other "unfamiliar affections" and relationships all cooperate in the establishment of what editors like to call "the authority of the text."

But this final Auden example graphically reveals the ambiguity in a concept like the authority of the text. The work we know as "September 1, 1939" exists in print in several different versions, and one of these is an absent text (as it were), a suppressed poem. Current anthologies of poetry which print selections from Auden choose between these different versions in definite and particular ways. When this happens, an editorial decision intervenes to assume some authority over the text. In fact, the assumption of authority over texts by later editors (scholarly or otherwise) goes on all the time, and the example from Auden, like the other examples I have set forth here, merely calls attention to the situation. Editors and textual critics are naturally aware of their interventions.

Nevertheless, the concept of the critical edition, so called, clearly induces the illusion among scholars that the chief obstacles standing in the way of the reconstitution of an original text lie in the past, with its accumulated corruptions and interfering processes. The critical editor enters to remove those obstacles and recover the authoritative original. The previous examples show, however, that such a scholarly project must be prepared to accept an initial (and insurmountable) limit: that a definitive text, like the author's final intentions, may not exist, may never have existed, and may never exist at any future time. Editors and textual critics may have to confront—do in fact confront all the time—a specific number of different early texts, or versions, which incorporate a now historically removed process of production and reproduction from which one can choose as a base text one of a number of optional versions.

But the examples show a further and related limit which scholarly editors in particular are faced with. When preparing a critical edition the editor chooses one particular version as the basis for his reading text, and he lets the critical apparatus carry all the information necessary for the reconstruction of other possible versions and reading texts. If we think of the literary work as a physical object, as a book with particular sorts of content that come first to the attention of our eyes and then of our minds, we may begin to see what a peculiar version of the "original work" is being presented to us in critical editions. Editors, including critical editors, exercise authority over their texts, and sometimes exercise a great deal of authority. But this is an obligation of their work, and it can no more be evaded than it ought to be obscured beneath illusory ideas about critical objectivity, final intentions, and authoritative texts.[83]

The critical edition is a historical edition, as we are often reminded. This means that (a) the method of investigating the text is carried out along historical lines, and (b) the actual edition will present, in its formatting operations, the evidence showing the historical development of the work from its originary moment to the present. The text it asks us to read is not a historically removed text at all, and the version which it chooses as the basis of that text—that is, the version which will organize our experience of all the complex textual data—is but one among several which could have been chosen. That choice will be based upon two dialectically related factors: the obligations placed upon the present by the authority of past events, and the demands made upon the past by present requirements. Furthermore, both of these factors will be defined in the actual practise of a particular scholar. The entire situation is nicely illustrated in the following example.

E. H. Coleridge's widely used critical edition of Coleridge's *Poetical Works* is based on the 1834 text of the work we know as "Allegoric Vision." The choice is not particularly remarkable since the 1834 text certainly represents the author's final intentions with respect to this work. Because of certain textual problems, however, E. H. Coleridge was forced to preface his printed text with a long editorial note, the most essential features of which I quote.

> The "Allegoric Vision" dates from August, 1795. It served as a kind of preface or prologue to Coleridge's first Theological Lecture on "The Origin of Evil. The Necessity of Revelation deduced from the Nature of Man. An Examination and Defence of the Mosaic Dispensation." . . . The purport of these Lectures was to uphold the golden mean of Unitarian orthodoxy as opposed to the Church on the one hand, and infidelity or materialism on the other. "Superstition" stood for and symbolized the Church of England. Sixteen years later this opening portion of an unpublished Lecture was rewritten and printed in *The Courier* (Aug. 31, 1811), with the heading "An Allegoric Vision: Superstition, Religion, Atheism". The attack was now diverted from the Church of England to the Church of Rome. "Men clad in black robes," intent on gathering in their Tenths, become "men clothed in ceremonial robes, who with menacing countenances drag some reluctant victim to a vast idol, framed of iron bars intercrossed which formed

at the same time an immense cage, and yet represented
the form of a human Colossus. At the base of the statue
I saw engraved the words 'To Dominic holy and merci-
ful, the preventer and avenger of Soul-murder.'" The
vision was turned into a political *jeu d'esprit* levelled at
the aiders and abettors of Catholic Emancipation. . . . .
A third adaptation of the "Allegorical Vision" was affixed
to the Introduction to *A Lay Sermon . . .* which was
published in 1817. The first fifty-six lines, which contain
a description of Italian mountain scenery, were entirely
new, but the rest of the "Vision" is an amended and
softened reproduction of the preface to the Lecture of
1795. The moral he desires to point is the "falsehood of
extremes."[84]

The situation we have here is interesting because it clarifies
two of the most vexing problems which preoccupy contemporary textual critics: the problem of choosing between textual versions, on the one hand, and the problem of the appli-
cable limits of a concept of authorial intentions, whether "original" or "final." In actual editorial practice, these two problems are normally brought into a close analytic relation with
each other, so that—typically, for example—the problem of
choosing which optional version of a text to print will be
decided by a search for "the author's final intentions". This
example graphically illustrates the problems which arise for
an editor when he operates with such guidelines.

The example is even more important, however, for what
it shows when an editor actively seeks to deal with the problem of a work's textual instabilities. The editor's note cuts
across the reading text which he presents and forces us to
read the work in the context of its many shifting original
shapes. This is, quite literally, not a text which ever existed
before; it is the (historicist) reconstruction by E. H. Coleridge
of poetical work by S. T. Coleridge (in which "work" is to be

understood as a process or as a specific series of related textual events, but not as a "text"). Furthermore, it is a reconstruction carried out according to a determinate structure, a text established in a particular point of view. "Allegoric Vision" exists in various textual versions, but the "Allegoric Vision" presented in E. H. Coleridge's edition forces us to regard all these texts as variants, or really functions, of the 1834 text. We see the work as Protean, but always from a particular vantage.

The example interests me, then, because it shows how every textual formation—including the critical works of scholarly editors who operate on shape-shifting texts like "Allegoric Vision"—necessarily reflects a special set of literary productive relations. The critical edition is so to speak a "genre" among texts; as such it is marked by peculiar characteristics and biases toward the original work which it seeks to reproduce, and these peculiarities are themselves historically determined (and hence historically explicable). Furthermore, any actual edition produced by a critical scholar will bear within itself yet other, and more particular, idiosyncracies which are characteristic of the scholar who produced it, and the context in which he worked.

What is especially important for us to see about the critical edition is its aspiration to transcend the historical exigencies to which all texts are subject. A critical edition is a kind of text which does not seek to reproduce a particular past text, but rather to reconstitute for the reader, in a single text, the entire history of the work as it has emerged into the present. To the scholar's eye, the critical edition is the still point in the turning world of texts, a text which would arrest, and even reverse, the processes of textual change and corruption. As such, the critical edition embodies a practical goal which can be (within limits) accomplished, but it equally embodies an illusion about its own historicity (or lack thereof). According to this view of itself, the critical text is reproduced with a minimum of interference by contemporary concerns on the one hand, and a maximum of attention to the historically removed materials on the other. The rules for producing critical editions place such emphasis on these matters that editors cannot be encouraged to reflect upon the contemporary motivating factors which operate in their work.

The theory of the modernized or nonspecialist edition enters the field at this point—Edmund Wilson's notorious, splenetic protest is an actual instance of such an intervention—to provide models for directing critical attention toward those contemporary motivating factors. A theory of textual criticism cannot be completed until the relationships of specialist and non-specialist editions are elucidated. These relationships are the subject of the next section of this essay. The presentation will complete the final phase of the argument, since the theory of such editions holds the key for elucidating certain important obscurities in the practice of modern textual scholarship.[85] In particular, I shall argue that the best scholarly editions establish their texts according to a catholic set of guidelines and priorities whose relative authority shifts and alters under changing circumstances. The value of a particular piece of work will be judged by the skill with which the editor is able to assess those circumstances. This skill, I hasten to add, is not an abstract or critically indeterminate set of powers. Rather, it is a function of particular social conditions and needs, and manifests itself in the scholar's ability to produce a text—whether critical or non-critical—which responds in an illuminating and useful way to those particular conditions and needs.

8. Modernized Editions and the Theory of Textual Criticism

When critics speak of the tasks of editing, they normally make a sharp distinction between the scholarly or critical edition on the one hand, and modernized or noncritical editions on the other. Some critics, like Bowers, have seen no real justification for modernized editions but the common view is that such editions often serve useful purposes. R. C. Bald's comments are persuasive.

> There will always be, one hopes, editions in modern spelling of the major English authors since Spenser. Chaucer can only be modernized by altering his language, and Spenser, with his deliberately cultivated archaisms, is also separated from us by a linguistic gulf, narrow and easily crossed, but none the less real. But if ever the day comes when no modernized editions of Shakespeare and Donne and Milton are available to the general reader, our cultural heritage will be in a sad state. The responsibility of the editor of a text in modern spelling is no less than that of him who edits in the old spelling; if anything it is greater.[86]

Bald's remarks suggest that good nonspecialist editions can involve as much scholarly intelligence as critical editions, or even more, precisely because the editor of a nonspecialized text is required to incorporate in the reading text alone a process of historical translation analogous to what the scholar sets forth through his critical apparatus. Talbot Donaldson's justly acclaimed modernized edition of Chaucer could not have been produced except by an editor possessing immense scholarly knowledge and skills. Narrower scholars than Donaldson or Bald often assign special value to the work that goes into the production of critical editions, and while it is right to demand that nonspecialist editions should be based on careful scholarship, we cannot forget that critical editions are always produced under the pressure of contemporary demands. The nonspecialist editor is perforce highly conscious of such demands, whereas the critical editor, because of the more specialized nature of his projects, tends to overlook them—and to overlook not merely the fact of them, but their fundamental relevance to his work.[87] Consequently, critical editors take it as a matter of course that their scholarly methods can judge the editorial work that produces modernized texts, but they rarely see that the theory and methods of nonspecialist editing might be necessary to pass a corresponding judgment upon the work of critical editors.

Just these scholarly considerations were present in the mind of Stephen Booth when he produced his excellent edition of Shakespeare's sonnets.[88] Throughout his preface he discusses the complex problems which a contemporary reader of the sonnets must face, and he sets forth his own rationale for dealing with those problems. His edition prints in parallel texts a facsimile of the 1609 Quarto version and a modernized version based on the following attitudes, goals, and scholarly assessments.

> My primary purpose in the present edition is to provide a text that will give a modern reader as much as I can resurrect of a Renaissance reader's experience of the 1609 Quarto; it is, after all, the sonnets we have and not some hypothetical originals that we value. I have

adopted no editorial principle beyond that of trying to adapt a modern reader—with his assumptions about idiom, spelling, and punctuation—and the 1609 text to one another. I do not modernize for the sake of modernizing or retain Quarto readings for the sake of retention, and I do nothing for the sake of methodical purity (to do that would be to let the means justify the end, and, since my modern text is physically coupled to the Quarto text reprinted in parallel with it, my lack of systematic rigor about particulars should not inconvenience anyone). Both my text and my commentary are determined by what I think a Renaissance reader would have thought as he moved from line to line and sonnet to sonnet in the Quarto. I make no major substantial emendations and few minor ones. It might therefore seem reasonable to reprint the Quarto text alone and simply comment on that, but the effects of almost four centuries are such that a modern reader faced with the Quarto text sees something that is effectively very different from what a seventeenth-century reader saw. (ix)

These remarks show an admirable sense of the problems which arise when old texts place demands on the scholar which collide with his obligations to his immediate audience. Booth is well aware, in fact, that his attempt to translate the early seventeenth-century text into an equivalent twentieth-century medium and format must often encounter insurmountable obstacles. These situations impel him to a parallel text edition, and the following explanation: that those passages and lines "resistant to translation into the twentieth century are accompanied by the Quarto text itself and by commentary that attempts to mark each unsatisfactory compromise for what it is" (xvi).

A recent paper by Thomas Greene enters an important critique of Booth"s attempt to produce a modernized text of the sonnets. "Anti-Hermeneutics: The Case of Shakespeare's Sonnet 129" argues generally against Booth's modernizing impulses, and specifically against the modernizations proposed for Sonnet 129.[89] Greene's argument is particularly interesting because his position is based upon an appeal to hermeneutics rather than to textual criticism. Modernization is, in Greene's view, "anti-hermeneutical" because it eases the contemporary reader's access to the work. In Greene's view, the 1609 text is much to be preferred precisely because it is more "difficult" for a twentieth-century reader, because it encourages and promotes interpretive action. Where Booth, like most editors of the sonnets, sees anachronistic accidentals of various kinds, or positive errors of substance, Greene stands resolutely for the principle of *difficilior lectio*.

The problem of line 11 focuses the whole set of issues. Like most previous editors, Booth introduces serious emendations into the line, which in his text reads: "A bliss in proof, and proved, a very woe," whereas 1609 reads: "A blisse in proofe and proud and very wo." To emend the line as Booth does is to rationalize what appear to be irrelevant anachronisms and positive errors. But Greene's argument is that this is merely a modern form of bowdlerizing, and that the line's obscurities may merely reflect our ignorance of older usages. Greene encourages us to think that perhaps the orthography of "proud" involves a punning device, and to take the absence of punctuation as a positive benefit to the line's operation. In this respect Greene stands opposed to the entire view which Booth takes of the sonnets and which is epitomized in the following set of remarks:

Dutiful retention of the Quarto's random use of italics

> (as in the Quarto text of sonnet 1, line 2) results in . . .
> distortions by giving the sort of urgency orthographic
> emphases give to *Adolescent* prose. Renaissance texts
> do make purposeful use of such devices (e.g. *Will* in the
> Q text of 135.1, 2, 11, 12 and 14), but they do not do so
> consistently (e.g. *will* in the Q text of 135.4, 5, 6, 7, 8,
> and 12 and *Statues* in the Q text of 55.5). The literary
> experience of Shakespeare's contemporaries, not condi-
> tioned to look for meaning in orthographic variations,
> presumably let them recognize orthographic signals
> when their import assisted what was inherent in the
> rhythm and sense of a line but let them ignore ortho-
> graphic peculiarities where they seem accidental; experi-
> ence presumably also let them ignore the absence of
> such signals in situations where they are appropriate,
> and presumably preserved them from our modern temp-
> tation to study a printer's use or non-use of capitals and
> italics as a clue to what a Renaissance writer wished to
> convey. In modernizing the Q text I have used roman
> throughout and have not used informative capitals
> because where they are not unnecessary they are unwar-
> ranted. (xvii-xviii)

But in fact we do not know so much about "the literary
experience of Shakespeare's contemporaries" to take such
positions, or to say, specifically, that they were "not condi-
tioned to look for meaning in orthographic variations." Scholarly opinion varies as wildly about the extent of
Shakespeare's involvement with the text of 1609 as it does
about the reliability of the text itself. As our scholarly
knowledge increases, however, we often discover that texts
which had previously seemed corrupt are not so at all; that it
is we (or our ignorance) who are at fault.

I instance this example of a scholarly disagreement not to
adjudicate the specific issue, however, but to dramatize why

and how textual critics and scholars involve themselves in matters of contemporary significance. A historical approach to literature, including a historical approach to the establishment of the texts of literary works, asks for a critical assessment of the textual traditions which we are instituting as much as it does of the tradition which we receive. This means that a critical edition has to include in its theory and historical procedures the capacity for an objective self-analysis. Such objectivity is made possible when the critical edition studies itself from the vantage that calls forth the nonspecialist edition, which is to say from a vantage of textual criticism that transcends both. Ideally, a critical edition should not be produced, and ought not to be evaluated, without situating it clearly in terms of its present orientation and set of purposes.

This general rule merely extends what has already been said about the nonautonomy of the authors and works we inherit from the past. Literary production is not an autonomous and self-reflexive activity; it is a social and an institutional event. Critical editions serve important functions within the institution and are themselves literary productions of a special sort. What they do—what they actually produce—reflects (as Byron's original texts are said to reflect) the producers' aims and purposes toward their contemporary institutional situation. Critical editors and theorists are normally quite self-conscious about their aims and purposes toward their received texts, but they have given much less attention to this other, equally significant aspect of their work. Nonetheless, although the theory has not elucidated these matters sufficiently, the editorial practice always takes them into account, however unselfconsciously.

We commonly observe the critical editor's self-conscious analysis of his current institutional obligations at the outset of the typical "Editorial Introduction." Here is where the editor will normally provide a brief textual history of the work. This history establishes the grounds of justification for the critical edition, that is, it serves to explain why the editor has thought it necessary to produce the edition at the present time. Here we observe, in its clearest form, the presence and operation of the theory of the nonspecialist edition in the production of critical texts: contemporary needs call out and define the character of the edition. The edition is not adequately explained if it is explained only in terms of its technical operations and methods of procedure, any more than a poem or creative work can be adequately explained in what have been called "intrinsic" terms.

These matters are plain enough. The issues become complex, however, when we focus once again upon the problem of choosing versions and copy-texts for critical editions of modern works. As Zeller and others have been able to show, when an editor faces the work he has to do, his initial textual analysis will reveal a number of possible texts which might reasonably be chosen. The question remains posed (and it is a question which neither Zeller nor anyone else who follows his revisionary approach has thus far been able to answer in theoretical terms): how does one adjudicate the different options? What principles (or theory), if any, should guide or determine the choice?

Certain critics and editors, like Donaldson, seem fundamentally opposed to theoretical and systematic guidelines, and hence argue that the problems have to be decided in purely pragmatic terms, ad hoc.[90] Critics who follow the dominant line developed by Bowers, as we have seen, are guided by the rule of final intentions, and the more traditional approaches taken by Thorpe and Gaskell, while they disagree with the dominant line in certain tactical matters, also agree that the rule of final intentions will govern. Their agreement here reflects a common descent from an earlier line epitomized in the Lachmann Method. Only Zeller argues that the rule of intentions (whether original or final) is impossible to follow under certain circumstances: "It is the difficulty, indeed the impossibility, of obtaining a text attributable exclusively to the author, when conditions are really complicated, which led Thorpe towards a recognition of an aggregate of alien influences."[91] And it is Thorpe's recognition which leads Zeller to the theory of textual versions, and hence to the problem stated above: on what basis does one make choices when the rule of final intentions cannot be applied—or, indeed, when no encompassing rule can be appealed to?

Before answering this question let me recall a few matters which we have already dealt with, but which will assume particular importance, once again, in the present discussion. In the first place, when Zeller, in the last quoted passage, speaks of "an aggregate of alien influences," we must be certain to purge his remarks of any suggestion that the institutional forces operating within literary works are in themselves "alien influences." Of course, whenever information is mediated some contamination results; this is the law of information theory which necessitates textual criticism. But a process of mediation is essential to literary production; indeed, many variant processes are necessary because literary works are only material things to the degree that they are social projects which seek to adapt and modify themselves circumstantially. As soon as an author utters or writes down his work, even for the first time, a mediation has to some degree come between or "interfered with" the original, unmediated "text."

A Romantic observer of this process like Shelley found it to be a matter of disappointment.

When composition begins, inspiration is already on the

decline, and the most glorious poetry that has ever been communicated to the world is probably a feeble shadow of the original conception of the Poet.[92]

Nevertheless, and as we have already seen, the literary work is always produced under institutional conditions—these vary with period and place—and their impact upon the author's work in the literary production is by no means always an alien or contaminating influence. Quite the contrary is the case. Of course, Shelley (and others) have sometimes lamented the fatality of all mediations, whether systematic or institutional, as "a necessity only imposed by the limitedness of the poetical faculty itself."[93] In such a (Romantic) view—and it is a view that continues to exercise its influence, even, as we see, in the domain of "rational" and "scientific" textual criticism—mediation processes are regarded as structural contaminants on an original and autonomous authority, and their effects have to be removed. In the present view, these mediations are regarded as conditions of being rather than otherwise; limits, if you will, but limits only as the body is a "limit" of humanness.

In the second place, we must recall that "conditions [get] really complicated" when we have to deal with texts which descend to us in multiple legitimate versions. This situation appears most dramatically in the modern periods, when the preservation of texts became such a scholarly imperative that critical editors typically are asked to deal with works which have been preserved in massive (sometimes complete) documented forms. The authoritative originals are not missing, and so many legitimate variant textual formations exist that the very concept of final intentions often proves helpless as a guide to choice.

We can now return to our question. I propose a guide which will not lead the editor to imagine that his work aims at definitiveness. The very existence of multiple versions is a limiting fact of the editorial situation which conditions the nature of the "choice" involved. We are dealing with a both/and, not an either/or, situation. This being the case, no amount of scrupulousness in examining the received documents will in itself decide the issue, for the rule of choice does not lie hidden in the documents. It lies hidden in the exigencies of the present and the future.

The rule emerges when we theorize on the practice of the nonspecialist or modernizing editor, whose choice of reading text is guided by what he judges to be most useful and important for a certain audience of readers. His task is to preserve the continuity of a more or less significant cultural resource. Such an editor is aware from the start of the multiplicity of legitimate texts because he is conscious of the multiplicity of audiences, among whom the original author and work are and have been continuously dispersed. From the point of view of the nonspecialist editor, there is no such thing as final intentions, whether authorial or otherwise. We recall once again Greg's shrewd comment: "Authority is never absolute, but only relative."

Faced with the existence of multiple legitimate options, the critical editor should not seek to impose upon them a system which pretends to distinguish one, ideal eclectic text. Rather, he must come to a judgment about which of the legitimate texts to choose given the demands which are made upon the work from the following quarters: (a) the current state of textual criticism in general, both as to theory and as to practice; (b) the current understanding of the textual history of the work in question, including its composition, production, reproduction, and reception histories; (c) the deficiencies which current critical practice has served to promote and (finally) reveal in the received texts; (d) the purposes of the critical edition's text, both immediate and projected.

The guidelines do no more than make explicit what has been governing the practice of many recent editors whenever circumstances were affected by massive textual documentation. The well-known cases of "La Belle Dame Sans Merci," which exists in two legitimate versions, and *The Prelude*, which also comes to us in two—or, as we now judge, in three—distinct constitutions, exemplify the situations which have governed practice. Critical editors have produced first one, then the other version, and eventually some produced editions with both. In Byron's case, works like "To the Po" have come to us in particular textual versions which are by no means definitive. Until the present Oxford English Texts edition, "To the Po" and a number of other famous poems were constituted in a series of texts based upon Byron's earliest manuscript copies rather than on his later manuscripts. More than one hundred and fifty years of readers have added their weight of legitimacy to these versions, which are in fact perfectly acceptable basic texts. Nevertheless, the later manuscript texts clearly have a prima facie claim to legitimacy which is all the more imperative at the present time, given the textual history of the poems to date. The choices of version and copy-text in the OET were guided by these considerations.[94]

The case of *The Giaour* is perhaps even more instructive since the optional texts are distinguished by different systems of punctuation where the final intentions of the author—or even of the author working cooperatively with his publisher—are not definable in any clear way. The best options range between the following choices: (a) the rhetorically punctuated first edition, which one would emend for later substantive corrections and additions (the copy-texts for the additional passages would be Byron's press copy manuscripts in order to remain as close as possible to the rhetorical style of the first edition's punctuation); (b) the more strictly and syntactically punctuated seventh edition, where the poem was first published complete, and which Byron proofed, with substantive emendations from later texts as necessary; (c) the third or the fifth editions, emended as in (a) above, which observe punctuation systems that strike compromises between options (a) and (b); (d) the thirteenth edition, which was carefully repunctuated for the first collected edition of Byron's works, though Byron did not proof this edition, with standard emendations; (e) the text printed in the first comprehensive collected edition (published posthumously in 1832-33 under the supervision of Byron's closest literary associates), again with the standard emendations; (f) a text based solely on the fair copy manuscripts, with standard emendations.

The argument developed in the present essay should explain why (c) through (f) eliminated themselves fairly quickly. The nature of the edition being undertaken, which will serve as the basis for many derivative texts for years to come; the character of the audience of the edition, which is both scholarly and—particularly through the derivative editions—more general; the historically received text, which has never been submitted to a thorough critical editing, or a careful analysis of textual options; the early printing history of *The Giaour*, along with the general character of Byron's relation to his audience and his publisher (so different from Shelley's); and, finally, the current state of textual criticism (both its limits and its powers) as I understand these matters: all these factors combined to make options (c) through (f) less desirable than either (a) or (b). My preferred text would have been with options (a) and (b) on facing pages, but the exigencies of the whole edition obviated this possibility. I finally chose option (b) because option (a) seemed a too specialized and artificial text.

Giving up the rule of final intentions and adopting instead a set of interconnected guidelines for choosing which texts they will edit, critics introduce a subjective factor into the critical process. Zeller's concept of textual versions adds to the danger posed by this subjective factor, since the concept of versions does not in itself judge the relative value of the different versions. It merely seeks to distinguish them. Consequently, since we do not have a nonsubjective means of deciding their relative value—since we have only a set of guidelines which have to be weighed and implemented by a fallible editor—the possibility exists of making a bad choice among the optional versions.

Donaldson once pleaded eloquently for the subjective factor in editing, and he denounced, with amiable severity, the entire project of a "scientific" textual criticism.[95] We may perhaps theorize his polemic and argue that, in problem-solving situations, the possibility of error must exist if the possibility of truth is to remain. The rule is a corollary of the principle of falsifiability. In the present instance, these considerations lead us to the conclusion that a systematic criticism has to be developed which has factored in an antisystematic element. Hence the re-emergence of a "subjectivity" within the present proposals.

Its necessity is seen if we compare the problems of editing Shelley and Byron in critical texts. Though they were contemporaries as well as friends, though they shared a number of the same habits of composition, and punctuated their manuscripts in similar ways, each requires a distinct and pointedly divergent editorial approach. The different printing histories for each poet's works, contemporary and posthumous alike; the special differences between the development of Shelley's texts at the hands of later critics and the markedly different development of Byron's; and, finally, the peculiar differences between their poetic styles: these and other factors make it necessary for an editor to approach the works of each poet in a very different way, especially when handling the problem of copy-text.

Briefly, we may say that Shelley's manuscripts frequently assert a strong demand to be adopted as copy-text, whereas Byron's rarely do. The reason for this difference is partly a matter of the printing histories of each poet's works, and partly a matter of their different poetic modes. As to the latter, Byron's is typically neoclassical in form and verse-line structure, and prosaic or rhetorical in tone or style; Shelley's, by contrast, is typically symbolist in form and verse-line structure, and lyrical in tone or style. As a consequence, Shelley's syntaxes are more fluid, suggestive, and ambiguous than Byron's. Punctuation, in Shelley's verse, becomes an absolutely crucial matter, whereas in Byron's work alternative punctuations are common and present no great difficulties.

Previous editors of Shelley's works have exacerbated the difficulties in their responses to the editorial problems. Recognizing the problems which Shelley's syntaxes frequently posed, past editors and textual critics tended to intevene in Shelley's texts with "improvements," in the hope of bringing a particular form of order to the poet's ambiguously structured syntax. The recent OET edition has continued this line of approach; and while it can prove useful and has done so in dealing with certain particular textual cruxes, it is a procedure which has systematically disfigured Shelley's texts.[96] Byron's texts, by contrast, suffered no such systematic corruption of their punctuation simply because his punctuation and syntax never presented editors with anything more serious than local problems.

Though Shelley published in a fashion that was normal for his period, his work as an artist is much closer to Blake's or Dickinson's—from the point of view of the editor and textual critic—than it is to Byron's. This is a fact which an editor cannot fail to take account of, one way or another (that is to say, for better or for worse). It would be a disservice to Shelley's work, as well as to the justifiable expectations of present and future audiences, if a critical edition today neglected to consider, in the matter of copy-text, the sincerity and integrity of Shelley's manuscripts. In this respect Shelley's manuscripts are far more important than Byron's; indeed, a powerful case could be made for producing an edition of Shelley's *Complete Poetical Works* in which the copy-text for the poems would be, in almost all cases, the manuscripts.

Needless to say, this case would not be founded upon an appeal to the rule of final intentions, but to the actual "achieved results" of the previous texts, both manuscript and printed; and to the immediate requirements of Shelley's readers, who cannot at present rely upon the texts which have been placed in their hands.

9. Summary

The analysis is now complete, and we may therefore summarize our findings by moving back through the presentation in reverse order. In doing so we shall take up the three main topics we have been concerned with. These are the same topics which Tanselle, in a recent essay,[97] has also noted as the crucial ones with which contemporary critics have been concerned. Since my own position differs so sharply from Tanselle's on at least two of these subjects, and since Tanselle's views represent the most advanced and persuasive defense of the Bowers line, I shall use his summary as a convenient structure on which to hang my own.

"The first set of questions," Tanselle observes, "consists of the preliminary ones that any editor must decide at the outset, questions about what kind of edition is to be undertaken." That is to say, will the edition be scholarly or non-scholarly; and if it is to be the former, will it be a critical text or will it not? For Tanselle the issue here is straightforward:

> Pieces of writing to be presented as documents are most appropriately provided in noncritical texts, whereas those to be presented as finished works are most usefully offered in critical texts.
>
> This is really all that needs to be said in a general way about the choice among different kinds of editions—the absence of any reference to modernizing,

> to the nature of the intended audience, or to whether or
> not writings are "literary" being meant to suggest that
> these matters need not be taken into account. However,
> so much has been said about them—they have proved
> to be the most prominent red herrings of editorial
> debate—that it now seems impossible to pass over them
> with no comment at all. Regularizing and modernizing
> (their aims may be different, but they amount to the
> same thing) are ahistorical in orientation and therefore
> have no place in the historical approach to texts—which
> is to say, in scholarly editions. (61)

Tanselle's inability to see the pertinence of a more probing
theoretical examination of this topic is a sign that he does not
recognize the historical dimension of all literary productions,
including critical texts, modernized editions, and so forth.
Tanselle sees "regularizing and modernizing" as "ahistorical,"
that is, as interventions in the critical attempt to establish a
purely "historical" text. But he is mistaken in his implicit
assumption here. Every literary production is "ahistorical" in
the sense of Tanselle's usage, and a complete theory of textual
criticism, including a complete theory of a critical edition,
will not be developed until the contemporaneity of such editions is elucidated more clearly.

Tanselle says that

> The intended audience may indeed be a factor—for
> economic reasons—in deciding whether a detailed
> apparatus is to be published with the text; but there is
> no reason why it should be a factor in determining the
> treatment of the text itself. (61)

He immediately introduces an exception to this statement,
however, in a footnote: "Except for some of the earliest works
in a language, which might be said to require 'translation',

rather than simply 'modernization,' for the general reader." What Tanselle does not see is that the "treatment of the text" in *every* edition is powerfully determined by the "factor" of "the intended audience." A theory of modernized and nonspecialist editions is necessary to a full critical theory for precisely this reason: that the factor of the intended audience is easily seen in the modernized edition, whereas in the critical and scholarly edition it is buried under the critic's social and institutional ideology.[98]

"The second large group of questions," Tanselle says, "concerns the nature of authorial intention and how one is to handle the difficult distinction between intention and expectation" (62). Tanselle's position here is well-known and follows Bowers and others quite exactly. I shall not rehearse what I have already argued at some length, but will merely observe that Tanselle's concept of author's intentions, as well as the related concept of authorship itself, no longer help to clarify what transpires in the production of literary works.[99] When Gaskell and others argue that, in the modern periods, a first edition is normally a better choice for copy-text or base text than an author's manuscript, their position seems to me clearly more sound than Tanselle's and Bowers's, for it takes better account of the social dimension which surrounds the process of literary production. The problematic character of Tanselle's and Bowers's concepts here only becomes clearer when we retreat in time to consider, for example, medieval texts.

Finally, the "third of these large central questions" deals with Greg's theory of the copy-text, and in particular with "the problem of the so-called 'indifferent' variant."

> This problem has been much discussed under the guise
> of examining how to select a copy-text. It is not neces-
> sary to have a copy-text at all, of course, unless there are

in fact some indifferent variants. The reason so much
attention has focused on the choice of copy-text is not
that it is a necessary first step in critical editing but that
in most cases variants appearing to be indifferent do
seem to occur, so that one needs a principle for favoring
one text over another. As for a general rationale for
choosing a copy- text, one can draw on testimony from
all periods, as well as on common sense and everyday
experience, to show that texts can be expected to
deteriorate as they are transmitted. It follows, therefore,
that a copy-text should be an early text—one as near to
the author's manuscript as possible, if not that
manuscript itself—whenever the individual circumstances do not suggest a different text as the more
reasonable choice. When they do, then by all means
another text should be chosen. (64-65)

On these issues Tanselle's position is far more thoughtful,
persuasive, and flexible than that of most critics who have followed Bowers. What remains to be said, I think, is that
Tanselle's catholicity on this matter has led him to abandon
the aggressive positions once occupied by the Bowers
adherents. But Bowers himself—the most vigorous proponent
of the narrow application of the theory—abandoned his earlier fortifications, first in 1972 and then again in 1978.[100] All
that remains to be done here is to provide an explanation of
this process of retrenchment.

   Tanselle's remarks show that the theory of the copy-text
has been clarified by its having been subordinated to a more
comprehensive problem. The first consideration which the
critical editor must face is to distinguish textual versions and
not, as Bower has said, to choose copy-text.[101]

   Distinguishing versions centers in the analysis of the process of textual *transmission*; choosing copy-text, in the analysis
of the process of *literary production*. In each case, so-called

author's intentions is one of the factors to be weighed and studied. When choice of copy-text is being made, the crucial factor is to distinguish true errors and deteriorations from legitimately produced variants. In particular, what is at issue are those indifferent readings and whether their production must be conceptualized for the author alone, apart and isolated from the cooperative involvements with his or her chosen (and sometimes fated) institutions of literary production. My own opinion, of course, again differs from Tanselle and the Bowers line generally, since my view of the process of literary production is far more socialized than theirs.

10. Conclusion

The tradition of textual criticism upon which our own work is most immediately dependent began in the eighteenth-century and flowered in the nineteenth. Anyone today who picks up Eichhorn, Heyne, or Wolf and is not humbled by their breadth and spirit ought to be ashamed. The early history of philology and textual criticism demonstrates clearly, even in the work of relatively minor figures, that these scholars—far from betraying any pedantic narrowness or abstraction from the present by their immersion in the past—were fired with the belief that historical method had uncovered a whole new educational program whose immediate and future significance could scarcely be underestimated.

Textual criticism was an instrumental discipline within the large enterprise they called *Alterthumswissenschaft*, and while the subordinate program served the larger enterprise, the latter supplied the former with its governing context and raison d'être. The historical method demanded that the textual critic try to achieve as complete an imaginative recovery of his past author as was possible. To edit ancient texts required, first, that the entire cultural and historical context of the original work be recovered; second, that the entire critical history of the work also be explored and elucidated; and finally, that the work itself be reconstituted for the present in terms of these two historical matrices.

The study of the works of the ancients is certainly most fruitful when one concentrates not so much on *the works themselves* as on *the authors* and *the periods* from which the works come. Only this method can lead to a true philosophic knowledge of human beings, for this method obliges us to search out the character and the entire context of a nation, and to grasp all aspects of the subject in their comprehensive interrelationships. The struggle to gain this kind of knowledge (for no one alone can hope to see its fulfillment) must be called absolutely necessary for every human being.

(Die Betrachtung der Werke des Alterthums ist gewiss dann am fruchtbarsten, wenn man nicht sowohl auf *sie selbst* sieht, als auf *ihre Urheber* und die *Perioden,* aus denen jedes herstammt. Nur diese Betrachtungsart kann zu wahrer philosophischer Kenntniss des Menschen führen, insofern sie uns nöthigt den Zustand und die gänzliche Lage einer Nation zu erforschen und alle Seiten davon in ihrem grossen Zusammenhange aufzufassen. Das Streben nach einer solchen Kenntniss (da niemand eigentliche Vollendung derselben hoffen darf) kann man jedem Menschen . . . unentbehrlich nennen.)[102]

Clearing ancient texts of their accumulated errors was an operation which required at once great technical skill and purpose, as well as a deep and humane sympathy for the work. Both the material form of the work and its aesthetic force and meaning developed as a function of its imbedded social and cultural nature. To understand and appreciate Homer, or to edit his work, required that you study both with as full a sympathetic consciousness of the social context as it was possible to gain: because authors, their works, and their texts were not isolate phenomena. All were part of a continuing process, a changing and sometimes even a developing history of human events and purposes.

This view of scholarship and program of general education are based upon a paradigm which sees all human products in processive and diachronic terms.[103] The paradigm has controlled the work of textual criticism from its inception, and it operates to this day. The theory of copy-text and the rule of authorial intentions emerge from a critical analysis of problems that are peculiar to the study of certain dynamic human phenomena.

My own view, however, is that the lines of critical procedure developed largely out of Bowers represent specialized and very restrictive applications of the original historical paradigm. Faced with problems that are specially pertinent to early modern and modern texts, these approaches often develop useful ways for handling them. Yet the procedures have sometimes been urged not as tactics to be employed as needed, but as a general strategy for editing all texts. In this respect they offer themselves as more comprehensive developments of the original paradigm we receive through the work of men like Wolf and Eichhorn. In my view, however, these lines are not always a development or more comprehensive extension of the original approach; rather, they often seem much more narrow and restricted. In asking us to analyze textual problems—indeed, to decide the most basic textual issues—within a sharply restricted analytic field, these approaches have tended to suffocate textual studies as well as the larger enterprise of which they are a part. Essentially these lines ask critics and editors to view the dynamic evolution of literary works in a context evacuated of its complex human relations. The author's productive work and the institutions of reproduction are either divorced from each other by the analysis or they are set in a negative relationship. This view of the social structure of literary production forces the critic to study both the text and the meaning of the work in the narrowest possible context—that is to say, in a human space whose contextual dimensions are psychological and biographical, or at most professional.

This narrowing of the critical focus is not, of course, the arbitrary consequence of an ingrained or natural pedanty in the critics concerned. On the contrary, it results from the changing historical character of authorship from Shakespeare's day to our own period. Leigh Hunt once said that Wordsworth stood at the head of the profession of letters in his age. The remark revolted Byron, not merely because of its elevation of Wordsworth, but even more because of its view of authorship.

> Did you read Hunt's skimble-skamble about Wordsworth being at the head of his own *profession*, in the *eyes* of *those* who followed it? I thought that poetry was an *art*, or an *attribute*, and not a *profession*;—but be it one, is that ******** at the head of *your* profession in *your* eyes? I'll be cursed if he is of *mine*, or ever shall be.[104]

The ideology of authorship implicit in this statement is old-fashioned, not to say anachronistic, in Byron's period, when the profession of letters, which began to take shape in the eighteenth-century, reached an advanced level of development in people like Wordsworth, Coleridge, and Hunt. The profession emerges in a fully developed form in the later nineteenth-century and is officially recognized toward the end of the century with the passage of the copyright laws protecting authors and their property rights.

Nevertheless, although this historical development is noticeable and important, and although the specialized and technical focus of textual criticism reflects that development, literary works remain human products with the broadest cultural interests and relationships. That they enter general society through the mediation of complex publishing and academic institutions is a central fact, but hardly one which should lead to a narrowing of the critic's focus. Yet this is precisely what tends to happen when editing and textual criticism are pursued along certain lines which are now current.

The chief difficulties emerge when textual criticism has the effect of desocializing our historical view of the literary work. When we make decisions about the condition and significance of various texts on the simple criterion of author's (final) intentions we foster serious misconceptions about the nature of literary production. Too many relevant aspects of the literary work are de-emphasized, or even abstracted from the critical view altogether, when we operate on such a principle. F. A. Wolf worked at a relatively primitive state in the history of textual studies, but such an approach would have been inconceivable for him.

Of course, it may be objected that the rule of final intentions is only relevant to the determination of the copy-text, and that I am introducing problems which have no relation to the use of the rule or to the theory of copy-text in general. But this is not the case. The choice of copy-text can involve major practical decisions which far transcend indifferent readings, especially when the choice is tied to the pursuit of an eclectic text based upon an ideal of author's intentions, as is the case with the Bowers approach. Whatever the practical effect, a choice based upon this line of reasoning will involve maintaining certain theoretical confusions in the discipline of criticism. To determine copy-text and the rules for emendation on the elementary basis recommended by the Bowers line of reasoning is to make crucial textual decisions without taking adequate and systematic account of all the relevant factors. A hypnotic fascination with the isolated author has served to foster an overdetermined concept of authorship, but (reciprocally) an underdetermined concept of literary work.

Texts can and must be analyzed in such a way as to distinguish author's intentions toward the works, or the degree of revision and correction which the various texts display, both authorial and nonauthorial. But fundamental decisions about copy-text and base text should not be made solely on the basis of such an analysis—especially if the function of the analysis is simply to isolate the authorial intentions rather than to plunge into the phenomena to understand their meanings and textual significance. The textual critic must go between and behind such matters to determine the contexts which they helped to produce: "to grasp all aspects of the subject in their comprehensive interrelationships." The status of accidentals is not the same for all texts, partly because of differences between authors (Shelley versus Byron), partly because publishing conventions and techniques change with place and time, and partly because language itself changes along with the societies which use the language. The character of the accidentals, then, may help to determine copy-text in one case, but may prove to be little or no help at all in another. This is only to say that the theory of the copy-text, the guideline of accidentals, and the rule of final intentions are all useful analytic devices whose power can only be determined when their precise limits are clearly grasped. These devices form part of a much larger structure of critical analysis, they do not define that structure, not even at the micro (or text) level. To determine the physical appearance of the critical text—indeed, to understand what is involved in such an apparently pedantic task—requires the operation of a complex structure of analysis which considers the history of the text in relation to the related histories of its production, reproduction, and reception. We are asked as well to distinguish clearly between a history of transmission and a history of production. Finally, these special historical studies must be imbedded in the broad cultural contexts which alone can explain and elucidate them.

Appendix:
A Possible Objection

My critique of the rule of final intentions throughout this essay has been tied to a series of counter examples, the most important of which are brought forward to argue the collaborative or social nature of literary production. The issue here involves the rule developed by Bowers that when a choice is to be made between author's manuscript and first edition, the presumption will be in favor of the manuscript, since it contains what we know to be the author's (rather than someone else's) intentions toward accidentals and so-called indifferent readings. My argument has been that the presumption should lie with the first edition since it can be expected to contain what author and publishing institution together worked to put before the public.

A friendly critic has objected that this view lays itself open to attack by other sorts of counterexample.

> We know from Lawrence's career, for example, that the author can be a willing partner in a helpful process, a willing or passive partner in an unhelpful process, or an unwilling partner in a downright repressive process. Conventional house-styling by a printer, active editing by Edward Garnett, silent censorship by Martin Secker, suppression by magistrates, threats of libel by Heseltine—all these things argue in his case against the printed text being generally seen as representing a successful transmission operation.[105]

This is of course perfectly true, and one could accumulate a host of similar instances. John Cowper Powys's novel *A Glastonbury Romance* (1932) was threatened with a libel suit as soon as it was published in England (1933). Powys had used a number of real place names in his book, and a Somersetshire landowner—who was the owner of a place called Wookey Hole, which figures prominently in the novel—sued for damages. The consequence was that Powys's next novel, which had just been published in America (1934) and which also made extensive use of actual place names, underwent a last minute set of revisions in the English edition to avoid another such suit. The novel was published in England as *Jobber Skald* in 1935. Not until many years later did this work appear in England in its proper original version, with the original title of *Weymouth Sands* (1963). Powys himself urged and carried out the corrections, so that one must see *Jobber Skald* as his "final" intended version. Nevertheless, *Jobber Skald* is not the version of this work that any reasonable editor would produce.

The expurgation, suppression, and mutilation of texts occur all the time and for many sorts of reasons. Powys's magnum opus, *Porius*, has never been published in a proper text. The novel was held up by World War II, and when it finally could be published it had to be drastically cut back because the book was long and paper was short. *Porius* was finally published in 1951, but that book resembles only in the most remote way the original epic narrative on which Powys hoped to stake his fame.

Nevertheless, these sorts of examples go to the issue of textual versions rather than to the rationale of copy-text. When authors and publishing institutions collaborate, the works they bring out may be well or poorly produced. Not every critical edition is good simply because it is a critical edition. In choosing the textual version, the editor must examine carefully the early publishing history in order to arrive at a reasonable decision. No scholar—one would hope, no publisher—would today reprint the 1951 published text of *Porius*; what needs to be issued is the version of the novel which survives in Powys's typescript, carefully edited of course.

Having chosen that version—having decided, in Lawrence's case, to print an unexpurgated text of *The Rainbow*, or even perhaps the two volume version of *The Rainbow* and *Women in Love* (which Lawrence once expressed a desire to see published)—the critical editor then faces the issue of copy-text. Tanselle is quite right when he says that this issue centers on the question of indifferent readings, and that it must be separated entirely from the problem of textual versions. In practical terms—to take the example of *Porius* once again—the editor has to decide whether he will give authority over accidentals and indifferent readings to Powys's typescript or to the 1951 printed text when a choice is available. When there is no choice to be made—when we are dealing with the expurgated passages and have only the typescript to rely upon—obviously one prints the typescript and edits only for the mistakes. But when we are printing the bulk of this novel, we have a choice between the typescript and the 1951 text.

The copy-text for such an edition should be Powys's original printer's copy typescript. This is an opinion which most editors would hold, I suspect. I only wish to emphasize here that such a choice cannot really be justified by an appeal to final intentions, though Powys's original (but interrupted and deflected) intentions are an important factor in the analysis. The 1951 *Porius* is a compromise production arrived at by mutual agreement between Powys and his publisher. Had the war not been a factor in the production, one presumes that Powys's publisher would not have sought for such massive excisions and revisions, and that Powys would not have made them.

One would not wish to use the 1951 printed text to decide between indifferent readings because the proof corrections will often be affected by the larger "revisional" changes which the work underwent in its early production phase. The better move is to start with the original typescript and use the subsequent materials, including the 1951 printed text, to introduce whatever substantive and accidental changes seem best.

The point is that the decision on copy-text always involves many factors, and that "author's intentions" cannot be offered as the determining one for all cases. It is only one of many factors to be taken into account, and while in some cases it may and will determine the final decision, in many others it cannot and must not be forced to perform that function. In all cases many factors enter into the decision, and in each case one or another factor will be the determining one. But to see "author's intentions" as the basis for a "rationale of copy-text" is to confuse the issues involved.

Notes

1. Giorgio Pasquali, *Storia della tradizione e critica del testo*, 2d ed. (Firenze, 1952); M. L. West, *Textual Criticism and Editorial Technique* (Stuttgart, 1973).

2. Paul Maas, *Textual Criticism*, trans. Barbara Flowers (Oxford, 1958); Fredson Bowers, *Bibliography and Textual Criticism* (Oxford, 1964) and his earlier *Textual and Literary Criticism* (Cambridge, 1959); James Thorpe, *Principles of Textual Criticism* (San Marino, Ca., 1972). A good survey of the field of textual criticism and editorial methods can be found in the CEAA/CSE *Introductory Statement* (Modern Language Association of America, April 1977), 3. This 20-page document was subsequently reprinted in *PMLA* 92 (1977), 586-97. It includes a useful bibliographical essay which surveys the significant work in the field to 1977. The bibliography may be supplemented by the checklist "Textual Studies in the Novel," *Studies in the Novel* 7 (1975), 446-60 as well as by G. Thomas Tanselle, "Recent Editorial Discussion and the Central Questions of Editing," *Studies in Bibliography* 34 (1980), 23-65. The issues with which the present monograph is concerned center in the controversies which have surrounded the work of the CEAA/CSE (the literature on this topic is surveyed in the *Introductory Statement*, 13-14). Tom Davis has written an important review article in which the *Introductory Statement* is critically examined: "The CEAA and Modern Textual Editing," *Library*, 5th Series 32 (1977), 61-74. See also the CEAA/CSE's manual *Statement of Editorial Principles and Procedures*, rev. ed. (New York, 1972) and *The Aims and Methods of Scholarship in Modern Languages and Literatures*, rev. ed., ed. James Thorpe (New York, 1970).

3. Edmund Wilson's famous attack originally appeared in two articles in *New York Review of Books* in 1968, and these were reprinted as *The Fruits of the MLA* (New York, 1968). Wilson's polemic served to focus attention on the subject.

4. The reader should consult the CEAA/CSE's *Introductory Statement*, cited above, for a good survey of the critical materials. I would also call attention particularly to the following more recent works: Tom Davis and Susan Hamlyn, "What Do We Do When Two Texts Differ? *She Stoops To Conquer* and Textual Criticism," *Evidence in Literary Scholarship: Essays in Honor of James Marshall Osborne*, eds. Rene Wellek and Alvaro Ribiero (Oxford, 1979), 263-79; Philip Gaskell, *From Writer to Reader* (Oxford, 1978), esp. chaps. 2, 5, 11, 12; Jane Millgate, "The Limits of Editing: The Problems of Scott's *The Siege of Malta*," *Bulletin of Research in the Humanities* 82 (1979), 190-212; and David Foxon, "Greg's 'Rationale' and the Editing of Pope," *Library*, 5th Series 33 (1978), 119-24.

5. The initiating article in this interesting controversy was Michael J. Warren's "Quarto and Folio *King Lear* and the Interpretation of Albany and Edgar," which was delivered in 1976 at the International Shakespeare Association Congress, Washington D.C., and later published in *Shakespeare Pattern of Excelling Nature*," ed. David Bevington and Jay L. Halio (Newark, Del., 1978), 95-107. In my discussions below I do not deal with my two central subjects, authorial autonomy and final intentions, in terms of the problems which appear in Elizabethan plays, and in dramatic works generally. The problematic nature of both concepts leaps to view when we study these sorts of text, as much recent work has shown. Commenting on two of the most important of these recent works, Stephen Orgel has observed "how much the creation of a play was a collaborative process, with the author by no means at the center of the collaboration"; and also, "that the notion of final or complete versions assumed by virtually all modern editors of Shakespeare is inconsistent with everything we know...about Renaissance theatrical practice" ("What is a Text?", *Research Opportunities in Renaissance Drama* 24 [1981], 3, 6. Orgel is here commenting on two of the most significant works which take up these matters, G. E. Bentley's *The Profession of Dramatist in Shakespeare's Time* (Princeton,

1971) and E. A. J. Honigmann's *The Stability of Shakespeare's Text* (Lincoln, Neb., 1965). The reader should also consider the implications of Steven Urkowitz's *Shakespeare's Revision of King Lear* (Princeton, 1980), as well as various recent scholarly works put out by Michael Warren and Peter Blayney, among others.

6. For a good survey of the history of Shakespearean criticism see *Shakespeare. The Critical Heritage*, ed. Brian Vickers (London, 1974-79), Vols. 1-6, including the useful bibliographies and introductions where the standard works on the history of the textual criticism are cited. For an introduction to the so-called New Bibliography see F. P. Wilson, "Shakespeare and the New Bibliography," in *The Bibliographical Society 1892-1942: Studies in Retrospect*, ed. F. C. Francis (London, 1945), 76-135. This essay was reprinted (and revised) as *Shakespeare and the New Bibliography*, rev. and ed. Helen Gardner (Oxford, 1970).

7. Randall McLeod's paper "The Marriage of Good and Bad Quartos" is a witty and provocative critique of the dominant critical methodology; McLeod uses the texts of *Romeo and Juliet* to exemplify its argument. The paper was delivered at the 1981 World Shakespeare Congress, and it will be published in *Shakespeare Quarterly.*

8. See Fredson Bowers, "Some Principles for Scholarly Editions of Nineteenth-Century American Authors," *Studies in Bibliography* 17 (1976), 223-28; my text here is quoted from the reprint of this article in *Bibliography and Textual Criticism*, ed. O. M. Brack and Warner Barnes (Chicago, 1969), 197-98. Philip Gaskell, *A New Introduction to Bibliography* (Oxford, 1972), 340.

9. CEAA/CSE, *Introductory Statement*, 3.

10. For a survey of recent critical work see *Textual Strategies*, ed. Josué V. Harari (Ithaca, 1979), and see especially the bibliography, 443-63.

11. Important works in this field are J. E. Sandys's *History of Classical Scholarship* 3 vols. (Cambridge, 1908; reprinted, New York, 1958); E. J. Kenney, *The Classical Text* (Berkeley, 1974); Rudolph Pfeiffer, *The History of Classical Scholarship*, vol. 1

(Oxford, 1968), Vol. 2 (Oxford, 1976). Also important are the series of reviews and essays (some still unpublished) by Anthony Grafton, and in particular "The Origins of Scholarship," *American Scholar* 48 (1979), 236-61; "From Politian to Pasquali," *Journal of Roman Studies* 67 (1977), 171-76; "*Prolegomena* to Friedrich August Wolf," *Journal of the Warburg and Courtauld Institutes* 44 (1981), 101-29; and the still unpublished "Polyhistor into *Philolog*: Notes on the Transformation of German Classical Scholarship, 1780-1850." The literature on biblical scholarship is vast and complex; good surveys in English of New Testament scholarship are Bruce M. Metzger, *The Text of the New Testament* (Oxford, 1968), and the study by Werner G. Kümmel, *The New Testament: The History of the Investigation of its Problems* (Nashville and New York, 1972). Old Testament scholarship is surveyed in R. H. Pfeiffer's *Introduction to the Old Testament* (New York, 1948), E. G. Kraeling's *The Old Testament Since the Reformation* (New York, 1955), and H.-J. Kraus's *Geschichte der historisch-kritischen Erforschung des Alten Testaments* (Neukirchen Kreis Moers, 1956).

12. F. A. Wolf, *Prolegomena ad Homerum*, 3d ed., ed. R. Peppmüller (Halle, 1884), 87-88.

13. The formulation is variously made: author's intentions, author's original intentions, author's final intentions. These different formulations reflect differences in the subject matter being discussed and will be elucidated below. Suffice it to say here that the first is a general formulation of wide applicability. James Thorpe's statement is typical of this usage: "The ideal of textual criticism is to present the text which the author intended" (*Principles of Textual Criticism* [San Marino, Ca., 1972], 50). The second form emerged (and is still used) when the authorial texts are distanced from their scribal or typographical copies, and especially when the authorial documents are no longer extant. The third formulation came into use when editors were dealing with heavily documented works, especially works which are preserved in one or more prepublication forms.

The literature on the question of final intentions is conveniently surveyed in G. Thomas Tanselle's "The Editorial Problem of Final Authorial Intentions," *SB* (1976), 167-211; reprinted in Tanselle's *Selected Studies in Bibliography* (Charlottesville, Va., 1979), 309-54. This may be supplemented by Tanselle's essay "Recent Editorial

Discussion," *ibid.*, esp. 52-57 and 62-64

14. For accounts of Lachmann and his methods see Sebastiano Timpanaro, *La Genesi del metodo del Lachmann* (Florence, 1963); F. X. Polzl, *Uber Karl Lachmann* (Vienna, 1889); Kümmel, 146-49. Pasquali's *Storia della Tradizione* is a brilliant critique of some weaknesses in the method as it is developed for classical texts.

15. In this context the names of Greg, Pollard, and McKerrow become important. But from the point of view of the subsequent development of Shakespearean textual criticism, the key document is W. W. Greg, "The Rationale of Copy-Text," *SB* 3 (1950-51), 19-36; reprinted in *The Collected Papers of Sir Walter W. Greg*, ed. J. C. Maxwell (Oxford, 1966), 374-91. (The latter text of this essay will henceforth be cited as "Rationale.") Greg's distinction between "substantives" and "accidentals" has come under some justifiable criticism. I shall adhere to the terminology in this essay for the convenience of my general argument. Greg's famous essay cannot be mentioned without calling to mind Fredson Bowers, whose important interpretation of Greg's essay led to his edition of *The Dramatic Works of Thomas Dekker* (Cambridge, 1953-61), the first edition to be produced through a systematic application of Greg's principles.

16. *Johnson on Shakespeare*, vol. 1, ed. Arthur Sherbo, with an Introduction by Bertrand Bronson (New Haven, 1968), 51-52.

17. This difference was early recognized by the New Bibliographers. See R. B. McKerrow's *Prolegomena for the Oxford Shakespeare* (Oxford, 1939) and Fredson Bowers's recapitulation in *On Editing Shakespeare and the Elizabethan Dramatists* (Philadelphia, 1955), 83-86.

18. See especially McKerrow, *Prolegomena*, and A. W. Pollard, *Shakespeare's Folios and Quartos . . .* (London, 1909), and W. W. Greg, *The Editorial Problem in Shakespeare* (Oxford, 1942; rev. ed., 1950). See also Richard Hosley, Richard Knowles, and Ruth McGugan, *Shakespeare Variorum Handbook: A Manual of Editorial Practice* (New York, 1971).

19. Brack and Barnes, *Bibliography*, 194-201.

20. *Ibid.*, 197-98.

21. *Ibid.*, 198-99.

22. The term is Bowers's: *ibid.*, 198.

23. See Bowers's *Textual and Literary Criticism*, where the method of subtraction is clearly formulated. In Bowers's words, we must seek to "restore the shape of the lost [original] manuscript as we strip away . . . the veil of print" (81). What is stripped away is the compositorial element in the printed texts.

24. G. Thomas Tanselle, "Greg's Theory of Copy-Text and the Editing of American Literature," *SB* 28 (1975), 167-229; reprinted in Tanselle's *Selected Studies*, 245-308. The latter text will be cited here.

25. James Thorpe, *Principles of Textual Criticism*; Philip Gaskell, *A New Introduction to Bibliography*; Donald Pizer, "On the Editing of Modern American Texts," *Bulletin of the New York Public Library* 75 (1971), 147-53. Gaskell and Thorpe dissent from within, however, in the sense that they share the heritage of the genealogical method and the New Bibliography, as well as a commitment to certain crucial concepts, like the ideal of authorial intention. Another critique from within can be observed in the work of George Kane and E. Talbot Donaldson. Kane and Donaldson emphasize "subjectivity" in the editing process where Bowers emphasizes system and theory. See *Piers Plowman: The B Version*, ed. George Kane and E. Talbot Donaldson (London, 1975), 130-31 and 212-13. The most significant departure from the Bowers line to date has been Hans Zeller's "A New Approach to the Critical Constitution of Literary Texts," *SB* 28 (1975), 231-64. The fact that this paper was first printed in English in Bowers's journal testifies to the intellectual vigor and purity which has always characterized Bowers's work.

26. Although Morse Peckham's essay "Reflections on the Foundations of Modern Textual Editing," (*Proof* 1 [1971], 122-55) was an attempt to deal with the issues theoretically, his way of

proceeding—via communications theory and psychology—seems to me to have missed the crucial issues by eliding the social and historical perspective.

27. Greg, "Rationale," 374. For some further discussion of the term copy-text see Paul Baender, "The Meaning of Copy- Text," *SB* 22 (1969), 311-18, and G. Thomas Tanselle, "The Meaning of Copy-Text: A Further Note," *SB* 23 (1970), 191-96.

28. Greg, "Rationale," 375.

29. Ibid., 376.

30. Ibid., 377.

31. Ibid., 381-82. The crux here is the status of the so-called indifferent readings." See the more developed discussion below, pp. 9-64, 113-15.

32. Ibid., 375, 380.

33. Ibid., 382, 384-85, 386.

34. Tanselle, "Recent Editorial Discussion," 64.

35. Ibid.

36. Peter Blayney, "Greg's 'Rationale,' Copy-Text, and Textual Theories," 1-2.

37. Greg, "Rationale," 384.

38. Ibid., 374.

39. Ibid., 376.

40. It seems odd that critics have not been more alive to the fferences between the textual-critical problems which are characristic of Shakespearean studies and the analogous problems in ore modern works. Bowers and the New Bibliographers were well

aware of the differences between Shakespearean problems and classical problems (see n. 17 above). The differences between the publishers and printers of the nineteenth and twentieth centuries and those of the Elizabethan and neoclassical periods are very great—in their levels of skill and standardized procedure, in their possession of more efficient technologies, and in the more professional and intimate relations they maintained with their authors. See Gaskell's remark quoted above, p. 58. As Gaskell suggests, these differences should not permit critics to treat the problem of accidentals in modern works with an approach designed for the treatment of an Elizabethan situation. The method of punctuating modern printed texts can hardly be seen as a contamination process in itself at all, given the sort of supervision which accompanies the printing of nineteenth- and twentieth-century books by author, publisher, and both in concert.

41. See Zeller, "A New Approach."

42. Tanselle, *Selected Studies*, 314. This formulation, I should point out, differs significantly from Bowers. In a letter to me Tanselle has pointed out "that your interpretation [of the phrase] is not what I had in mind. . . . I used the wording . . . only because a critical text will not normally coincide with any single preserved document. . . . I did not mean that phraseology to imply acceptance—as a general rule—of the kinds of alterations made in a publishing office. . . ."

43. The problem here reveals itself in the illustrations provided by Hershel Parker in his interesting essay "Melville and the Concept of 'Author's Final Intentions,'" *Proof* 1 (1971), 156-68.

44. Tanselle, *Selected Studies*, 283-84.

45. Greg, "Rationale," 384.

46. Brack and Barnes, *Bibliography*, 195.

47. "Current Theories of Copy-Text, with an Illustration from Dryden," *Modern Philology* 68 (1950), 19-36.

48. An interesting critique of the concept of "substantive edition" may be found in Fredson Bowers, "McKerrow, Greg, and 'Substantive Edition'," *Library* 5th Series 33 (1978), 83-107.

49. Tanselle, *Selected Studies*, 330.

50. Ibid., 332.

51. Gaskell, *A New Introduction to Bibliography, 340.*

52. Tanselle, *Selected Studies*, 330.

53. Ibid., 300.

54. Thorpe, *Principles of Textual Criticism*, 48. But see the discussion below, pp. 81-94, 100-9.

55. *Blake. Complete Writings*, ed. Geoffrey Keynes (Oxford, 1966), 207-8.

56. Ibid., 820, 865 (letters of 30 Jan. 1803 and 19 Dec. 1808).

57. Ibid., 867.

58. *Byron's Complete Poetical Works*, ed. P. E. More (Cambridge, Mass., 1905), v.

59. Tanselle, *Selected Studies*, 284.

60. See Foxon's discussion of these matters in his essay cited above, note 4.

61. See *Byron's Don Juan. A Variorum Edition*, vol. 1, ed. T. G. Steffan and W. W. Pratt (Austin, Tex., 1957), 176-78.

62. *The Autobiography of Malcolm X* and similar works raise the problem of the authority of the ghost writer. See below pp. 85-86.

63. See Chaucer's "To His Scribe Adam," in *Chaucer's Poetry. An Anthology for the Modern Reader*, ed. E. Talbot Donaldson (New York, 1958), 542.

64. Tanselle, *Selected Studies*, 339.

65. The term "ideal text" should not be confused with the technical term from bibliography of "ideal copy". For a good discussion of the latter see G.Thomas Tanselle, "The Concept of Ideal Copy," *SB* 33 (1980), 18-53.

66. The complexity of the problems in establishing an orderly recension for the *Piers Plowman* manuscripts is so great that Kane was forced to abandon the genealogical approach. His remarks on the state of the *A* manuscripts are noteworthy: "recension is not a practicable method for the editor of the *A* manuscripts. Nor is the creation of a hierarchy, with some one copy elevated to the role of authority: while some of these manuscripts are more corrupt than others, all are corrupt to an indeterminate but evidently considerable extent" (*Piers Plowman: The A Version* [London, 1960], 115).

67. Gaskell, *A New Introduction to Bibliography*, 337.

68. Byron's intentions toward all aspects of his various works shifted with time and circumstances, nor does his case seem, in this respect, untypical of most authors. Byron is particularly interesting because his shifting intentions are often explicitly tied up with non subjective factors of different kinds.

69. Zeller, "A New Approach," 240.

70. The best statement of Bédier's position—the most finished form of his views—is set forth in his late, two-part essay "La tradition manuscrite du *Lai de L'Ombre*," *Romania* 54 (1928), 161-96, 321-56. See also A. E. Housman's classic essay "The Application of Thought to Textual Criticism," *Proceedings of the Classical Association* 18 (1921), 67-84.

71. *The Works of Sir Thomas Malory*, vol. 1, ed. Eugen Vinaver (Oxford, 1947), xcii.

72. Tanselle has already urged that this concept of definitiveness is untenable and should be eschewed ("Greg's Theory of Copy-Text and the Editing of American Literature").

73. See *Lord Byron. The Complete Poetical Works*, vol. 3, ed. Jerome J. McGann (Oxford, 1981), 86-87, 424-25.

74. See *The Complete Works of Walter Savage Landor. Poems*, vol. 15, ed. Stephen Wheeler (London, 1927-36), 401.

75. R. H. Super, *The Publication of Landor's Works* (London, 1954).

76. See John Halberstadt, "The Making of Thomas Wolfe's Posthumous Novels," *Yale Review* (Autumn, 1980), 79-94, and the exchanges between Halberstadt and Richard Kennedy in *New York Review of Books* of 16 June 1981 and 19 March 1981.

77. A. C. Swinburne, *Lesbia Brandon*, ed. Randolph Hughes (London, 1952).

78. Vinaver, *Malory.*, xcv.

79. Ibid., civ.

80. See Edward George Bulwer-Lytton, *Pelham* . . . , ed. Jerome J. McGann (Lincoln, Neb., 1972), xxvii.

81. Joseph Warren Beach, *The Making of the Auden Canon* (Minneapolis, 1957), 22.

82. *Collected Poems of W. H. Auden*, ed. Edward Mendelson (New York, 1976); see the Editor's Preface, 11.

83. Randall McLeod has an amusing (but trenchant) essay called "UnEditing Shak-speare," *Sub-Stance* 33/34 (1982), 28-55 which bears on the topic. He shows how crucial the physical form of a work can be, how a work's meaning may depend as much upon its format and physical constitution as it does on its words.

84. *Coleridge. Poetical Works*, ed. E. H. Coleridge (Oxford, reprinted 1967), 589-90.

85. See Lorene Pouncey, "The Fallacy of the Ideal Copy," *Library*, 5th Series 33 (1978), 108-18. I disagree with a number of this essay's positions, but its discussion nicely highlights the place which modernized editions ought to have in the mind of the critical editor.

86. R. C. Bald, "Editorial Problems—A Preliminary Survey," in *Art and Error: Modern Textual Editing*, ed. Ronald Gottesman and Scott Bennett (London, 1970), 42. The article appeared originally in *SB* 3 (1950-51), 13-17. For Bowers's view see Brack and Barnes, *Bibliography*, 194-95: "One may flatly assert that any text that is modernized can never pretend to be scholarly, no matter at what audience it is aimed." But Bowers is less obdurate on the subject elsewhere: see *On Editing Shakespeare*, 69.

87. Various attacks upon the CEAA editions were grounded in an awareness of the scholar's obligations (his scholarly obligations) to a more general audience—obligations which are all the more pressing when classic American works are involved. The general point concealed in this situation is that all literary works, including scholarly editions, are produced in a functional relation to a public, and their value is partly to be measured by this relationship. Audiences vary, of course, and some scholarly works are produced for a very small circle of scholars. The point is simply that the theory of a critical edition must make its assumptions about the audience an explicit part of the theory.

88. *Shakespeare's Sonnets*, edited with an analytic commentary by Stephen Booth (New Haven, 1977). Pages cited in the text are to this edition. Booth's fine edition should be supplemented with the indispensable New Variorum Edition of Hyder Rollins, *Shakespeare The Sonnets* 2 vols. (Philadelphia, 1944).

89. Greene's paper was given as a lecture at Johns Hopkins University in 1981 and again at California Institute of Technology in 1982; it is published in *Poetic Traditions of the English Renaissance*

ed. Maynard Mack and George deForest Lord (New Haven, Conn., 1982), 143-62. Its views converge in certain important ways with those of Randall McLeod's "Unemending Shakespeare's Sonnet 111," *SEL* 21 (1981), 75-96.

90. E. Talbot Donaldson, *Speaking of Chaucer* (London, 1970), 102-18.

91. Zeller, "A New Approach," 249.

92. "A Defence of Poetry," in *Shelley's Prose*, rev. ed., ed. David Lee Clark (Albuquerque, 1966), 294.

93. Ibid.

94. That is to say, it was not guided by the appeal to final intentions, although one might easily be led to think so, in the present climate of critical opinion, since the OET texts are based—in these cases—on texts which Bowers would approve. The point is that the two best optional texts of "To the Po" possess, in my view, the status of versions (in Zeller's sense of that term). An editor therefore cannot choose between them on the rule of final intentions, but must establish other grounds for a choice.

95. See Donaldson's discussion in *Speaking of Chaucer*, 102-18.

96. Kenneth N. Cameron's review of the OET Shelley (vol. I) gives a good brief discussion of the issues and problems: see *Studies in Romanticism* 12 (1973), 693-99.

97. Tanselle, "Recent Editorial Discussion," 23-65. Page references to this essay will be given in parentheses in the text.

98. What I mean here may be clarified through the following remark by Pierre Machery on the nature of idelogy: "Like a planet revolving around an absent sun, an ideology is made out of what it does not mention." It exists, he goes on to say, "because there are things which must not be spoken of"—or, I should add, which have not been spoken of, or (sometimes) which cannot be spoken of. See *A Theory of Literary Production* (London, 1978), 132.

99. That is to say, its original usefulness has been exhausted as the field of study has developed itself and—in this process—has laid bare the obscurities inherent in the concept as it was originally formulated.

100. See Bowers's essays "Multiple Authority: New Problems and Concepts of Copy-Text," *Library* 5th Series 27 (1972), 81-115, and "Greg's 'Rationale of Copy-text' Revisited," *SB* 31 (1978), 90-161.

101. See Bowers's essay cited in note 18 above.

102. The passage is from Wilhelm von Homboldt; it is quoted by Wolf in his *Darstellung der Alterthums-Wissenschaft* (1807), in the *Kleine Schriften*, vol 2, ed. G. Bernhardy (Halle, 1869), 884-85n.

103. I am using the term "paradigm" here in the context of Thomas Kuhn's writings on the history of science. Margaret Masterman's essay "The Nature of a Paradigm" discusses the emergence, elaboration, and collapse of paradigms in a way that I have found most useful. See *Criticism and the Growth of Knowledge*, ed. Imre Lakatos and Alan Musgrave (Cambridge, 1970), 59-90.

104. Byron's letter to Thomas Moore, 1 June 1818.

105. From Edward Brown's letter to me, June 1981.

Index